MILLIONS OF READERS HAVE WITNESSED THE STARTLING
REVELATIONS UNLOCKED IN THE PAGES OF HAL LIND-
SEY'S BOOKS—REVELATIONS THAT HAVE ALTERED FOR
ALL TIME THEIR VIEW OF THE WORLD AND THEIR FAITH
IN THE FUTURE.

Now, in this, his most important offering, mankind's
most pressing problems are faced and hope and faith
are rekindled.

THE LIBERATION OF PLANET EARTH

If you ever wanted an answer to the question
"What makes me tick?" this is the book
that will give it to you.

The Liberation of Planet Earth

Hal Lindsey

BANTAM BOOKS
TORONTO · NEW YORK · LONDON

This low-priced Bantam Book
has been completely reset in a type face
designed for easy reading, and was printed
from new plates. It contains the complete
text of the original hard-cover edition.
NOT ONE WORD HAS BEEN OMITTED.

THE LIBERATION OF PLANET EARTH
A Bantam Book / published by arrangement with
Zondervan Publishing House

PRINTING HISTORY
Zondervan edition published 1974
2nd printing .... August 1974
3rd printing .... October 1974
Bantam edition / January 1976
2nd printing .. November 1977   4th printing ...... October 1979
3rd printing .... July 1978   5th printing .... June 1980
6th printing .... October 1980

Bantam Books are published by Bantam Books, Inc. Its trade-
mark, consisting of the words "Bantam Books" and the por-
trayal of a bantam, is Registered in U.S. Patent and Trademark
Office and in other countries. Marca Registrada. Bantam
Books, Inc., 666 Fifth Avenue, New York, New York 10103.

PRINTED IN THE UNITED STATES OF AMERICA

15 14 13 12 11 10 9 8 7 6

DEDICATION

I dedicate this book to three very special gals in my life, my daughters Robin, Jenny, and Heidi. They've cheerfully given up overnight guests and parties, trips to Disneyland and the beach, and have spent many quiet hours playing because Daddy and Mom were working on "the book." Without this loving cooperation, *The Liberation of Planet Earth* might not have come into existence. Whatever blessing God may give as a result of this book, it's theirs to share for all eternity.

SPECIAL THANKS

There are three people who deserve special thanks for making this book a reality.

Minna Ratzlaff, Portland, Oregon. Minna took a series of my tapes which dealt with the subject of this book and typed them into rough transcripts. Then she sacrificially mimeographed these and gave them out by the thousands, and in so doing, God gave her a great personal outreach that only eternity will reveal.

Pete Gillquist, Grand Junction, Tennessee. Pete took time from his own busy writing career and spent many long weeks editing the rough transcripts into a workable manuscript and in so doing saved me many hours of work. Many thanks to you, Pete.

Jan Lindsey, Pacific Palisades, California. Little did my dear wife realize when she majored in English and minored in Journalism in college that one day God would team her up with a guy who could preach and teach, but needed someone to put it all down on paper. She's been an integral part of the writing of my last three books, and her practical insights into many of these great truths have been a tremendous ministry to thousands. Thank You Lord, for giving this woman to me.

Contents

Introduction

Introduction

You can buy transparent, ouchless, polkadotted and happy-faced Band-Aids in every size for every kind of hurt, except the kind of hurt that men have in their souls—a hurt that has spilled over to make an aching, wounded world.

That's not to say attempts haven't been made to put giant-sized bandages on the ills of mankind. One trip to a bookstore will reveal thousands of titles that promise a cure for loneliness, depression, sexual hangups, marital problems, mental illness, crime, wars, alcoholism, and myriads of other desperate ailments that afflict men today.

All these volumes have one thing in common. They agree that humanity is in trouble. But after that point, there's no accord as to what can be done about repairing these damaged lives.

My feeling is that you can't begin to prescribe an effective cure until you have an accurate diagnosis of the real nature of the problem. But how can we know where to look amid the books and voices spouting their "proven" cures for an accurate assessment of what ails men and women in our world today? We don't want to be taken in by promises of cheap remedies and halfway healings. Life is too short for that.

Somewhere in the midst of all this human chaos and confusion we've forgotten a very fundamental fact. All of creation seems to have a great unity, design, and purpose, and it's inconceivable to me that man should be an exception to this. There must have been an original meaning and purpose for him that got lost somewhere along the way and resulted in a morass of alienation, frustration, and hopelessness.

I've written this book to share how I was rescued from my own personal alienation from God, myself, and society and how I found the reason for why I had been put on this earth. My sincere hope is that any kindred souls who need forgiveness, encouragement, and hope will read these pages and find God's solution for their own lives.

THE LIBERATION OF
PLANET EARTH

Chapter One
A Candidate for a Miracle

A fourth-century philosopher, Augustine, said, "God, You have made us for Yourself, and our hearts are restless until they find their rest in You." I believe he was accurately describing the first twenty-five years of my life.

When I was a ten-year-old, living in Houston, Texas, I first began to ask the big question, "Is there really a God that a guy could know personally?" I was a normal kid with more than the usual amount of spunk. I gave my folks a lot of worries and headaches, and although our family life had its ups and downs we got along pretty well.

My folks weren't what you'd call regular church-goers. My mom periodically went and took me along with great reluctance on my part. I halfheartedly listened to the sermons, sort of hoping to find out if there was any way to feel closer to God (if He was real).

Misfire No. 1

At age twelve, seriously wanting to know God, I impulsively responded to a call to walk down to the front of the church and make a religious commitment. When I talked with the counselor he said, "Of course, you want to join the church."

I answered, "Well, if that's what you're supposed to do, I guess so."

He said, "Naturally, you'll want to be baptized."

"Well, yeah, I guess so," I replied.

Inside I thought, "Come on, tell me what this is all about." But nobody explained to me what a real commitment to Jesus was all about, at least not so I could understand it.

And so I went through the ritual of joining the church. I was baptized. But somehow all that got through to me was that I had now made a sort of New Year's resolution with God that I was going to try to do the best I could the rest of my life. And if my good deeds by the end of my life outweighed my bad deeds, somehow I'd make it.

Well, I really tried to stick with this new commitment and find some meaning in it. Yet after a few months I realized that if there was a God, I still didn't know Him. There was no reality of God or Jesus in my life. I kept going to church periodically, listening and trying to find out where I'd missed the boat.

Misfire No. 2

By the time I was fifteen I was extremely frustrated. There was conflict in my home and in my personal life, and I was becoming a very hostile young man. But I still had a deep sense of need to get on the right track with God, so I responded that year, in another church, to another invitation for those who wanted to know God to come to the front. It was a long walk down the aisle and I surely hoped it would work this time.

I wound up being told to join the church and be

baptized again. So I was baptized a second time, and after a few more months of stumbling around with no new reality of Jesus in my life, I said to myself, "You know, there must be something wrong with this whole business of walking to the front of a church, because it didn't take this time either."

In the particular churches I had attended, they emphasized that if you're a Christian, you don't drink, you don't smoke, you don't go to movies, and you don't dance. I had honestly tried to play the "Christian" game by their rules, so I didn't do any of these things. I was an athlete, and the coach didn't want us to drink or smoke anyway.

I soon began to realize that all the other guys my age were beginning to explore sex and booze and seemed to be having a great time while all I had to show for my "Christianity" was that I wished I could do what they were doing, but couldn't. I began to think, "I've got all the liabilities and none of the assets of this business of being a Christian." I was tired of God cramping my style so I began to stray away from the whole church scene.

Misfire No. 3

By the time I was seventeen though, I began to fight a great battle inside me. I started doing a lot of things everyone else was doing, but I gradually developed a deep sense of guilt. I was sure that if there was a God, He surely must be angry with me and probably wanted nothing to do with me.

In desperation I decided I'd give God one more chance because I really felt as if I needed to have my life cleaned up. I remember going to yet another church at the urging of a friend, and when the call was given to go forward, I headed for the front again, much to my friend's embarrassment. The personal worker who knelt to pray with me was no doubt very sincere and eager to get me into the fold, but he had no idea how to communicate with a high-geared teenager and I never did understand what it was all about. He finally got around to asking me to join the church and be baptized, so I went through the whole process a third time.

The Hardening Process Starts

Well, trip No. 3 didn't last very long. One thing I'd found out for certain was that simply going to the front of a church during an altar call and being baptized won't get your heart right with God. All these false starts eventually brought me to the point where I said, "I've got to be honest; I don't know if there is a God because I've gone looking for Him and haven't found Him. All religion has done is cramp my style. I'm just going to kiss it all off and live the way I want to."

And I did!

Systematically I began to harden my mind against God. I knew what I was doing, but I'd become very bitter and figured that I'd given God a chance at me and He'd muffed it. Now it was my turn to run my own life. And how I did run it! I pulled out all the stops. I started in big with booze and sex, and although my conscience did bother me at first, I finally got to where I could do those things with no conscious sense of guilt at all.

I entered the University of Houston, but partied my way out two years in a row. Uncle Sam wasn't impressed with my academic career and decided my talents could be put to better use in the army. I beat him to the punch, though, and joined the U.S. Coast Guard where I figured I'd never see much of the action in Korea.

I played every angle I could and wound up going to school the whole first year in special classes at the Coast Guard training school in Connecticut. During this time I really thought I'd reached the apex of living because I'd luckily taken up with some friends who had connections in New York City. I was running around with a guy whose father was vice-president of one of the largest corporations in America. He kept a suite of rooms at all times at a swank hotel in New York City, and he let us use them any time we went into town. Naturally I tried to pull liberty every week-end in New York City.

Would You Believe — Times Square?

One Saturday, after blowing my paycheck at a wild party the night before, I was standing on Times Square with another sailor and we were looking for someone to touch for a loan so we could eat. About three o'clock in the afternoon we finally decided no one was coming.

I looked across the street from Times Square and saw this sign that said "Free Food" in big letters. And in small letters underneath, it said "Jesus Saves." I nudged my buddy and said, "Let's go over and make those Holy Joes feed us—they ought to be good for something."

You see, by this time the contempt I had for God and religion was deeply ingrained in my behavior. But I figured I could swallow my antagonism long enough to get something to eat. We had finished our meal and were about to make a strategic withdrawal when a worker blocked our way and said to me, "Young man, are you a Christian?"

I didn't want to get into a hassle with the guy so I looked him straight in the eye and muttered through clenched teeth, "Well, I hope so." I thought that would get him off my back. But it didn't.

He said, "I can tell by your answer that you're not a Christian."

I shot back sarcastically, "How can you know that about somebody else? If there's anything I've found out about this whole religion business, it's that you can't be sure of anything."

But the man wasn't scared off, and he looked at me with real compassion and concern—and that got to me. He said, "I think I can understand why you might feel that way. Obviously you've never had it made clear to you why Jesus had to come into the world and what it is that He really offers you."

I nodded and said wryly, "That's for sure."

"You see, sailor," he went on, "you look as if you've

lived a pretty rough life. But with God it's not a matter of how bad you've been or even how good you've been. The only issue with God is whether you've come to see that when Jesus hung on that cross, God put all those sins of yours onto Him, and then Jesus took the punishment of death for those sins which should have fallen on you. Now He can offer you a gift of His love and forgiveness instead of His holy wrath. If you'll accept that forgiveness, it'll bring you to God and make Him real to you."

That was more than twenty years ago, but what he said to me that day was so clear and startling I can still remember essentially what it was.

Yet I had built such a wall around my heart that I wasn't ready to believe what he'd said. So I shoved the guy out of the way and walked out with a cynical laugh. As I left he fired a final statement at me that I never forgot: "Young man, you may reject me, but if you reject the gift of God's love, then His wrath will fall on you for all eternity."

That "shot" hit below the belt!

Off to the Mardi Gras

That was my only brush with spiritual things for the next five years. From Connecticut I was transferred to New Orleans, which I came to think was the swingingest place on earth. I was stationed there for about two years. I liked New Orleans so much that when I was discharged from the Coast Guard I decided to stay there. I lived near the French Quarter.

With the experience I'd gained in the Coast Guard, I got a job as a tugboat captain on the Mississippi. For almost four years I worked on the river. During this time I'd work a week, then have a week off. I hit New Orleans every other week with a full paycheck and a week in which to spend it. Every other week I'd drag back to the boat half dead and broke. Wow! I really thought I was living!

But in giving myself devoutly to wine, women, and

song, I began to find there were diminishing returns. The more I experimented with first one thing and then another, the less I was satisfied. Finally I got to the point in life where I began to ask, "What do you do for an encore?"

By now I was almost twenty-six years old. I began desperately grasping for something that might give some meaning to my life. Being the life of the party and the one no one ever took seriously was a role I increasingly hated. I started talking to people about their philosophies of life. I realized then how shallow I was. My playboy philosophy was to "live fast, play hard, die young, and leave a good-looking corpse."

I even began to be interested in talking to people about their ideas on religion. Everyone's ideas were so different, yet they all thought they were right. But they couldn't all be right. I came to the conclusion that everyone else was as mixed up as I was about religion.

Too Close For Comfort

One night while I was aboard ship, I had to make a crossing in a dense fog to take several oil drilling crews across the river. The fog was so thick you couldn't see the bow of the boat. I attempted to start up the generator and it wouldn't go. Without the generator you don't have radar, and without radar you don't know where you are on that river in the fog.

"We don't care what the risks are," the men said.

"Okay," I told them. "It's your neck." I pulled out a stopwatch and a compass and took off across the river.

All of a sudden my blood ran cold as I heard a steamship whistle just to my left. A big ship was coming right at us. I throttled. I couldn't see anything, but I could hear those big engines bearing down on me. Instinctively, and for no navigational reason, I whipped the wheel to the right and felt my boat just graze the side of the steamship. We slid along the side of it all the way back.

To this day I don't know how we made it. God was

really with me. Had we been hit broadside, it would
have cut our craft in two and sent it to the bottom
within seconds.

After that close call I started doing a lot of thinking
about death. Like a lot of people, I'd had thoughts of
taking my own life on several occasions, but the nagging fear of what might lie beyond the grave kept me
from it. I saw that night, however, that we all stand
just a breath away from death and it can find us even
if we're not looking for it.

That experience did a lot to sober me, and I can see
now that it was an important turning point in my life.

More Than Good Luck

Everything came to a head one night a few months
later. I tossed and turned on my bed; my head was
spinning with doubts and fears and questions. I had to
get some answers.

I remembered that I had a Bible in the bottom of my
seabag. I'd carried it for years as a good-luck charm—
like a rabbit's foot—but I'd never read it. I pulled it
out and began thumbing through it, and I found myself
really interested as I read a few things about the life of
Jesus. I decided right then that I would try to forget
everything I'd heard about Jesus from men and just try
to see what He said about Himself. I began reading at
the beginning of the New Testament—in the gospel of
Matthew.

To my surprise I ran into the Sermon on the Mount
in chapters five through seven. I'd never been too
excited about what I'd heard this Sermon contained.
The only part I remembered hearing was that if you
looked at a woman with lust in your mind, you'd already committed adultery with her in your heart.

There it was again, those same words, right in front
of me. I stopped and thought, "Man, who's got a
chance with a rule like that? And I haven't just been
lusting either!"

As I read on and saw all the other commandments

Jesus gave, I thought to myself, "Forget it, Lindsey. You haven't got a chance. You've broken every rule in the Book."

The New Beginning

Despondently I flipped over to another part of the New Testament—John, Chapter Three. As I glanced down the page I was intrigued by a conversation Jesus had with a man who was looking for answers about God, just as I had been for years. The man's name was Nicodemus, and Jesus told him that unless he was born again, he could never understand the kingdom of God or enter it.

"What's all this about being 'born again'?" I asked myself. "If there's anything I need, it's to be born all over again. I was surely born wrong the first time."

And you know, at that point the Spirit of God really began to work on me because my whole life seemed to flash before me. I remembered how I'd grown up grappling for the meaning of life, struggling to find God, with heartaches, emotional stresses, and a terrible self-image. I recalled my high school years and how I knew I basically had plenty of ability, but because I was so messed up emotionally I never finished anything I started. It seemed as if I just couldn't succeed. When I finished high school, I'm sure the senior class thought of me as the guy most likely to fail.

I saw that my whole life was the pattern of a loser, a guy with more than enough talent who never seemed to get it together. And I thought, "Man, it would be so wonderful to be able to start all over again—to wipe the slate clean and have a new life."

That's what being born again suggested to me— having a new life! Maybe the second time around I could get it all together. And yet, as Jesus talked about being born again, I couldn't see how something like that could ever happen to me. I figured I was too far gone.

As I read that third chapter of John over and over, it

finally dawned on me that all I had to do to be born
again was to *believe* that what Jesus did on the cross
was done for *me* personally.

Not the Praying Type

I really felt as if I wanted to pray, but I honestly didn't
know how. I simply said out loud, "God, if this is real,
then show me how to believe. I don't have any faith. I
don't even know if You're there."

The New Testament I had was one of those distrib-
uted by the Gideons to public school children. In the
back it said, "If you want to make a decision to believe in Jesus as your Savior, this is the way you do it."
It quoted the words of Jesus from Revelation 3:20,
"Behold, I stand at the door and knock; if any one
hears My voice and opens the door, I will come in to
him, and will dine with him and he with Me." It explained that the "door" is our will and we can choose
to invite Jesus Christ into our lives and accept the forgiveness for our sins that His death made available.

So I said, "God, if all this is real, then I want Jesus
Christ to come into my life. I really need to be forgiven.
If He can do that, then I accept Him right now. God,
please show me the truth."

The next morning, to my amazement, the first thing
I wanted to do when I awoke was read that Bible—
and that was something new! For the first time it really
began to make sense.

I returned to New Orleans after a couple of days and
went on my usual wild week-long tear. The only thing
was, this time it wasn't as big a kick as it had always
been.

That Fantastic Fanatic!

When I got back on board ship the next week, a deckhand came up to me and said, "Skipper, there's a new
boat-driver that tied up here and, man, is he crazy.
He's been down in the barroom every day—preaching."

"What in the world is he preaching about?" I said.

"About Jesus," he replied.

"Well, you tell him I'd like him to come aboard," I said. "I'd like to get some of his ideas about Jesus."

My deckhand looked at me as if *I'd* lost my mind.

The next day he brought the preacher aboard. The guy had heard about me and was a little uncomfortable. But I began to talk and he eased up.

"You know, a week ago something happened that I'd just like to get your opinion about. I understand you're a preacher."

He nodded and started rambling a bit. "This has been the wildest tour of duty I've ever had," he said. "I've got a wife and six kids over in Alabama and I couldn't get a job anywhere but here. I've been wondering what I'm doing here in this God-forsaken place."

I began to tell him my story. I told him about what I'd read in the Bible and how I'd prayed. This guy's mouth dropped open, then it got a little wider and a little wider, and I'll never forget what he first said to me.

"So *you're* the reason I couldn't get a job anywhere else."

"What do you mean by that?" I asked.

"Well, God wanted us to meet. He obviously sent me here to talk to you and let you know that you've done the right thing."

It turned out that he was an Assemblies of God preacher. He took the Bible and went through many parts that basically gave me the assurance that what I'd done was right. He talked to me about the importance of reading the Bible daily. By the time he was through, I knew Christ was in my life and that I had truly been born again. A couple of days later he left and I never saw him again.

That New Life Begins

I didn't start going to any church because I didn't know which one to go to, but I progressively began to notice changes taking place in my life. I became intensely

interested in reading the Bible, and without my trying
to reform myself, my inner desires about many things
began to change. I would slip down into my cabin to
read the Bible because I didn't want my crew to think
I'd flipped-out over religion. A lot of my friends began
to notice the change in my lifestyle and really began to
worry about me. They even brought a minister to talk
with me one day; he told me not to get all worked up
about the Bible.

Six months passed. I decided that the New Orleans
scene was not the most conducive to my living a Christian life, so I returned to my hometown of Houston. I
remember saying to myself, "Maybe I can find someone here who can tell me more about what the Bible
means." I knew I was on the right track, but I'd gotten
a late start and had to learn a lot in a hurry.

I worked at several different jobs, and I usually ate
my lunch alone and read the Bible. One day a fellow
worker noticed me and asked me if I wanted to come to
his church and hear a scholar speak on the Middle East
conflict (the Suez Crisis). He said the minister was
going to explain how the Bible had predicted much of
what was happening in the Middle East.

This really intrigued me, so I went with my friend.
The man spoke for two and a half hours, and I was so
excited I couldn't sleep that night. I literally stayed up
all night checking out what he had said, and by morning all those fulfilled prophecies had convinced me that
the Bible was really the inspired Word of God.

I began to go to this church and study under this
man's teaching. Without realizing what was happening,
I was studying the Bible about six to eight hours every
day and holding a full-time job at the same time. My
folks began to get a little worried about me becoming
overly zealous.

And a Child Shall Lead Them

Finally my dad came to me and said, "Hal, I remember
that when you were living in New Orleans, I came
over to visit you and you took me on a wild tour of the

French Quarter. I was shocked to see the way you were living. Now a year later you come home with a Bible under your arm and you're completely different. I don't know what's happened to you, but I'd surely like to."

I sat down and explained as best I could what had happened to me. To my amazement, tears came to his eyes. He said, "I'd like to know Jesus Christ like that."

We got on our knees in the front room, and he asked Christ to come into his life and be his Savior. My dad at age fifty-two became a newborn child of God, just like I had become. My mom still wasn't too sure about what was going on. She was a true believer in Jesus, but had never been taught anything about how to make the Christian life work day by day for her. Within a few months Jesus began to be real to her also.

Called to the Ministry

After about a year and a half of intensive Bible study in my church, God used a story from the Book of Exodus to show me the plan He had outlined for my life. He wanted me to teach His Word to others.

You can't imagine how shocked I was as I read the story of Moses at the burning bush and in no uncertain terms God said to me, "You're going to be another bush through which I'm going to speak."

The reason for my amazement was that I was scared to death to get up in front of people and speak. I'd quit a speech class at the university because I was terrified to open my mouth.

I told the Lord, "If You want to make a preacher out of me, You've got to perform a miracle on me first."

"That's no problem for Me," He said. "Look at the conversation I had with Moses in Exodus four. When I called Moses to go before Pharaoh and tell him to let My people go from their bondage in Egypt, look what he said to Me:

" 'Please, Lord, I have never been eloquent, neither recently nor in time past, nor since You have spoken to Your servant; for I am slow of speech and slow of tongue.'

"And this is what I, the God of the impossible, said to Moses: 'Who has made man's mouth? Or who makes him dumb or deaf, or seeing or blind? Is it not I, the LORD? Now then go, and I, even I, will be with your mouth and teach you what you are to say.' "

As I looked at those verses of Scripture and recalled the mighty way in which God had used Moses *after* this incident, I said, "Lord, You can do *anything*. If You made my mouth and You're calling me to use it for You, then You can put the words into it just as You did for Moses."

Trial Run

Shortly after this I was asked to teach an adult Bible class one Sunday. I almost said No when they asked me, but then I decided this was a good chance to give God an opportunity to put some of those words of His into my mouth.

I studied for days, and when I got up before the class it was with trembling knees but a bold heart that was putting all its confidence in God! To my amazement (Oh, me of *much* faith!) the people were really hit by what I said, and furthermore it was a terrific experience for me. Now and then during my lesson I'd start to remember where I was, and the old panic would begin inside me. Then I'd remember what God told Moses about putting His words into our mouths, and my heart would calm down.

After the class a woman came up to talk. I'd noticed her in the back of the room and she looked as if someone had been tromping on her toes all during my talk. She said, "Young man, I believe God has singled you out to teach His Word far and wide someday, but your grammar is so offensive that nobody is going to want to listen to you."

I knew she was right. I really murdered the King's English!

The World's Oldest Third Grader

"I'm an English teacher," she said, "If you'll come twice a week to my home, I'll teach you proper grammar."

I asked her why she was willing to do this.

"Because God told me to," she replied.

So I began to learn. She had to start back with third grade grammar; she brought me up to college level in a year. During this same period of my life I was really beginning to thrill at an expanded understanding of the Scriptures.

Hungry For the Word

As my knowledge of Scripture broadened, and the calling of God became clearer, I sensed more than ever my need to really *learn* God's Word. One night I said, "Lord, You know what I really want to do is go to seminary."

But how could I get accepted? Besides my sordid past and lack of any "religious credentials" whatever, I had never finished college. The school I wanted to attend was a four-year *graduate* school of theology, one of the toughest in the country.

God's answer came as He directed me to read one day in Psalm 71. I knew that these verses of Scripture, penned so many years ago by David, were God's mantle thrown upon me; for reasons known only to God, I was to be one of those who would somehow declare His power to my generation.

"O God, You have taught me from my youth; and I still declare Your wondrous deeds. And even when I am old and gray, *O God, do not forsake me, until I declare Your strength to this generation,* Your power to all who are to come.

"For Your righteousness, O God, reaches to the heavens, You who have done great things; O God, who is like You? You, who have showed me many troubles and distresses, will revive me again, and will bring me up again from the depths of the earth" (Psalm 71:17-20).

Since God was calling me to speak for Him; it only made sense that He would have to open the doors to seminary for me. When I realized this, I stopped worrying about how it was all going to come about and I just started trusting Him and making my plans to go.

Faithful is He Who Calls YOU

I submitted my application for seminary and I'm sure that when they received it, it took them two or three days just to stop laughing. There was virtually nothing on the form that would recommend me as a candidate for Dallas Theological Seminary.

Unknown to me, my pastor had made a special trip to the seminary to talk to the admissions director. "On paper this guy doesn't look like much," he told him, "but he's taught himself Greek on his own initiative, and he has a fire burning in his heart for God."

So they sent me an IQ test, and I knew my acceptance depended on my performance. I said, "Lord, I don't know what my IQ is (I knew my IQ score must have been low when I went into the service, because I'd taken the test with a terrible hangover), but I believe You can give me supernatural wisdom."

It was as though my mind had become a computer! I knew the hand of the Lord was on me, and I thought to myself as I whizzed through that test, "If I could think like this all the time, I'd be a genius." I finished way before the time limit. I went over the test again, correcting a few places, sealed it up, and sent it in.

In — By the Grace of God

I received an immediate reply: "You're accepted!" That miracle I'd been expecting had happened.

Here I was, accepted. But I was also flat broke! I'd been out of a job, laid off because of the 1958 recession.

I was sitting at home one afternoon. My mother came in and said, "Hal, you've got to write the seminary and tell them you can't come. We wish we had the money to help you, but right now it's just impossible for your dad and me to spare the money."

"Mom, God has called me to go to seminary and He's led those at Dallas to accept me. Now, *somehow* He's going to provide the money."

I remember going into my bedroom, closing the door, getting down on my face on the floor, and saying, "Okay, Lord. I said those words. Now You back me up!" While I was praying, my mother came into my room with some mail that had just arrived. "There are several letters here for you," she said.

Keep Those Cards and Letters Comin', Lord!

I opened the envelopes, and every one of them contained a check. I had not made my need known, yet many people said later that God had strangely placed within their hearts an urge to send money to help toward my seminary education. Letters began coming in nearly every day. By the time I left for Dallas I had enough money to go through the entire first year.

That's the way the Lord took me through four years of seminary. I never had any guaranteed income, but all my bills were paid by the time I graduated. That living by faith was good preparation for the ministry God was preparing me for.

Further Preparation For My Ministry

One of the greatest needs I'd begun to feel was for someone to share my life with. I'd had a heartbreaking experience with marriage when I was an unbeliever in New Orleans, and my wife had found someone she liked better and divorced me. I knew I needed a woman's love and companionship, but I was scared to death that it might blow up on me again. For this reason, although I was in my late twenties, I didn't date much during seminary. I really believed God had a woman of His choice somewhere for me and if I would simply wait for His best, He'd give her to me.

I knew that whoever He gave me would have to be someone very special to put up with me. She'd have to be mature and deeply committed to serving the Lord. I also thought it wouldn't hurt if she were pretty.

During the last part of my junior year at seminary, this very gal, Jan Houghton, walked quite unexpectedly into my life. We knew each other only five days before we both recognized we were the ones God had saved each other for.

Those five days were all we had together, for then she had to return to her ministry with Campus Crusade for Christ at Smith College in Northampton, Massachusetts. Three weeks later God unmistakably led me to call her and ask her to marry me. She'd already committed this to the Lord, and He gave her an immediate Yes.

Two months later, without our having seen each other once in between, Jan flew to Houston and married me. In the flesh we were total strangers, but we had the unmistakable mandate from God that we belonged to each other, and He had already given us a spiritual oneness.

Through the years that we've been married God has vindicated over and over the reasons He brought us together. We served Him as a team in Campus Crusade for many years after my seminary days, and now we work together in teaching and speaking around the country and in writing.

Summing it All Up

I hope by now you can see why I've exposed so much of my personal life to you. I've wanted you to see how God delights in taking very ordinary and sometimes messed-up lives and doing extraordinary things through them. Never in a thousand years would I have dreamed God would use me to write books that have sold in the millions and have brought life and hope to so many.

Me, who lived so hopelessly for so many years of my own life.

But that's God's peculiar delight—turning Simons into Peters, Sauls into Pauls, and messed-up men into vessels that can bring honor to Him.

In the chapters that follow I want with all my heart to help you see what it is that's done this to my life. I'm certainly no "finished product," and I'm daily being pruned by God to become more of what He wants me to be. But that too is an exciting process and one that's going on in all of us. Getting a better look at how God is refining us and how He's equipped us to live *above* our circumstances in this life makes the future something to look forward to rather than to dread.

If you want to move from the ranks of the ordinary into the world of unlimited possibilities, I challenge you to read on with an open heart and mind and you'll become a candidate for a miracle.

Chapter Two

What in the World Is Wrong With Man?

Any medical doctor worth his salt knows he can't bring about a cure for a disease unless he first diagnoses the problem correctly. Politicians and statesmen must carefully and accurately assess the underlying causes of problems in their town or state or country before they can pass effective legislation to correct matters.

The same is true when seeking to understand the most perplexing and challenging question of all time: "Why does man think and behave as he does?"

There's no shortage of diagnoses for why we do the things we do. Whole fields of scientific study are devoted to this question. Psychology tries to find out why *individuals* think and act the way they do. Sociology specializes in the dynamics of *group* behavior.

But whether you've got one man alone or a whole group together, almost all rational thinkers today are trying to come to grips with what's wrong with human behavior, what's wrong with our institutions and what's wrong with the world.

21

Man Seen as a Quirk of Evolution

One suggested answer to this problem was set forth by
Arthur Koestler in a talk given at the fourteenth Nobel
Symposium in Stockholm in 1969. He said, "There
have been many diagnostic attempts made to explain
man's abnormal behavior, from the Hebrew prophets
to contemporary ethologists [scientists who study animal behavior]. But none of them started with the
premise that man is an aberrant [abnormal] species,
suffering from a *biological* malfunction."

He asked the question, "Is our aggressiveness towards
our fellowmen socially acquired, or is it biologically
built in, part of our genetic makeup and evolutionary
heritage?"

Koestler pointed out that from the dawn of consciousness until the middle of the twentieth century,
man had to live with the prospect of his death as an
individual. But since the incredible forces of atomic
power were unlocked three decades ago, man now has
to live with the prospect of his death as a *species*.

Faced with this threat of self-extinction, one would
have expected man's aggressiveness to have become
tempered by reason.

"But," Koestler wrote, "appeals to reasonableness
have always fallen on deaf ears, for the simple reason
that man is not a reasonable being; nor are there any
indications that he is in the process of becoming one.

"On the contrary, the evidence seems to indicate that
at some point during the last explosive stages of the
evolution of Homo sapiens, something has gone wrong.
There is a flaw, some subtle engineering mistake built
into our native equipment which would account for the
paranoid streak running through our history." [1]

While one may not agree with all of Arthur
Koestler's conclusions, the fact remains that he too has
sought to give an explanation of man's deviant behavior and has concluded that we are stuck with a
genetical quirk of nature for which there is no hope of
remedy.

[1] *Los Angeles Times,* June 7, 1970.

Are We Ready to Go "Beyond Freedom and Dignity"?

B. F. Skinner, the author of the controversial book *Beyond Freedom and Dignity* and the man who is thought by many to be the most influential living American psychologist, has his theories about the nature of man and how he functions best, yet they are diametrically opposed to Arthur Koestler's. Koestler felt man's *internal* mechanism was defective and the cause of his malfunction, while Skinner feels the entire problem of man's errant behavior lies in the *external* influences that affect him daily.

Skinner's solution to self-centered behavior is to place sufficient control over a man's external conduct and culture until he no longer has any inner freedom or free will. In this tightly controlled environmental state, men will refrain from polluting, overpopulating, rioting, making war, being selfish, greedy, unloving and arrogant—*not* because of the disastrous results of these, but because he has been conditioned to want what serves the group interests.

This may sound a little like the supposed utopia of George Orwell's *1984,* but this thinking is no joke to Dr. Skinner. Because of his many experiments with the controlled behavior of animals (and to a lesser degree with humans) there are many reputable thinkers who have bought all or parts of this philosophy of behavioral control.

Although Skinner is strongly opposed by most humanists, religionists, and Freudian psychoanalysts, he steadfastly maintains that behavior is determined completely from without, *not* from within. He insists that any idea of a soul or inner man is a superstition that originated, like belief in God, from man's inability to understand his world and his own actions.

Two Opposing Camps

If we were to follow B. F. Skinner's philosophy to its inevitable conclusions, we would be forced to admit that no man is responsible for his failure to behave correctly. He could simply plead that he was never "conditioned" to do the right thing. This would perhaps result in removing all sense of personal guilt from man but it would also create civil and moral anarchy.

What we're really dealing with here in these two men's representative views are two completely opposing views of man and of why he behaves the way he does. They both agree that man has a behavioral problem, but one view says it's an inner problem and the other says it's external. Nevertheless, in both camps *no* appreciable solution to the dilemma of how to start man behaving in an unselfish, loving, peaceful, generous, kind, patient and concerned manner has been discovered.

Whatever Happened to "Sin"?

For years most psychiatrists and psychologists have dismissed the old-fashioned religious idea of "sin" as irrelevant at best and downright dangerous at its worst. They've accused religion of producing guilt in its followers and have counseled patients to cast off their guilt feelings and do what they want.

But now, one of the sacred inner circle of psychiatry has defected from his previously held views of why man behaves improperly. Dr. Karl Menninger, world-renowned psychiatrist, says in his new book *Whatever Became of Sin?* that mental health and moral health are identical and the only way our suffering, struggling, anxious society can hope to prevent mental ills is by recognizing the reality of sin.

"If the concept of personal responsibility and answerability for ourselves and for others were to return to common acceptance," he says, "and man once again would feel guilt for sins and repent and establish a conscience that would act as a deterrent for further sin, then hope would return to the world."

Tragically, Menninger says he was prompted to write his new book after speaking to a group of young liberal theologians and hearing them express their frustration and inadequacy to deal with the problems of their parishioners or compete with the evil forces attracting their young people.

"It came to me," Menninger said, "that our clergymen have become shaken reeds, smoking lamps, earthen vessels . . . spent arrows."

His solution is to stand up and tell the world what its problem is. "Preach it! Tell it like it is. Say it from the pulpits. Cry it from the housetops!" says Dr. Menninger, psychiatrist, *not* evangelist!

A Viable Alternative

Dr. Karl Menninger has not traded in his psychiatrist's couch for a pulpit, and certainly many people will find things in Menninger's views that they can't go along with completely, but he has done something many ministers have failed to do in our times. He's offered a diagnosis for man's problem which is the same one the Bible has taught. Man is a sinner and needs reconciliation with God, with his fellowman, and with himself.

Sin Has Caused a Barrier Between God and Man

I would like to assume that anyone reading this book has come with an open mind and wants to understand the Bible's diagnosis of the human dilemma.

From the first book of the Old Testament to the last book of the New Testament, there is one consistent theme and that is that God and man experience an alienation—a barrier, if you please—that man cannot remove and God says He already has.

Every error ever taught regarding man's relationship to God has historically begun with an improper understanding of sin and its devastating effect on man. There's no use talking about who Jesus was or why He came until we first understand the nature of the barrier that exists between man and his God.

If a couple came to me who were alienated from each other and had erected an insurmountable barrier between them, I could begin to help them resolve their conflict only when I got them to see how the barrier between them had come about.

The Universal Barrier — its Causes and Results

Picture if you will the first record we have of man's relationship with God. It was in a beautiful environment, and there was true fellowship and communication between God and man. Man was free to do as he wanted in all areas, but he was asked, as a free expression of love and obedience toward God, not to do one simple thing: don't eat of a certain tree in the garden.

Now that doesn't seem like much for God to ask. I often ask my children not to do certain things and I know that whether they obey me or not, to a certain degree, represents their love and trust of me. Because I love them I don't force their obedience, but I do desire it as a recognition that they respect my judgment above theirs—that what I've asked is only something for their best interest.

When Adam and Eve decided to take a bite of that forbidden fruit in defiance of God's command, their disobedience erected a barrier between themselves and God, and the fellowship they had been experiencing with their Creator was broken.

That story is recorded in the first book of the Bible, the Book of Genesis; in the other thirty-eight books of the Old Testament and the twenty-seven books of the New, we have the continuing story of what God has done to reconcile man to Himself by removing the barriers of separation.

The Fourfold Barrier

We can condense into four categories the blocks that we've erected one on top of the other in the barricade that separates man from God. This wall is so impenetrable that all the religions, philosophies, idealisms, good works, and ingenuity of men can't pull it down.

The compelling reason that made me write this book is to pass on the best news I have ever heard and that is that God Himself *has* torn down the barrier.

Let's look at the barrier first and then we can fully appreciate what it cost God to abolish it!

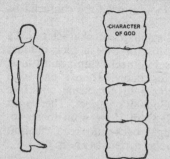

Chapter Three

Barrier Number One: God's Holy Character

Many of us know someone whose life is so pure and exemplary, who has such a goodness about him, that we're just a little uncomfortable in his presence. Especially if we have any idea that he knows about some of *our* grosser habits. We don't feel that way around most of our friends, though, because we know *they* live just like we do.

What do you suppose it is that makes us feel such a difference, almost an invisible barrier between that person and ourselves?

It's his saintly character.

We know we don't measure up to his standard of conduct, and we feel he might be inclined to be judgmental of us. So we feel an alienation of sorts.

To a much greater degree, that's the problem between God and man. The character of God is so flawless and the nature of man is so full of flaws that the very holiness of God becomes a barrier to man.

Now, before you say to yourself, "Well, it's God's fault, then, that man is alienated from Him. God needs

29

to lower His standards if He wants to reconcile with man," we need to take a look at what the character of God is really like.

We're talking about a standard of character that's way out of our league. Most of us can pick out ten people we know and measure ourselves up against their lives and not come off too badly. There's only one small problem when it comes to measuring ourselves against the character of God—it's perfect. There's no grading on the curve with God! If we want to be accepted by Him and brought back into reconciliation with Him, we must become as perfect as He is.

Impossible, you say?

Not so!

The story of how God went about making man acceptable again, after he lost his fellowship with God in the Garden of Eden, is the story we tell in this book. The first thing we must thoroughly understand is

The Character of God

These are the component parts of the character of God as He has revealed Himself in His Word and His history of dealing with men.

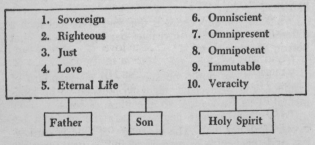

GOD IS

1. Sovereign	6. Omniscient
2. Righteous	7. Omnipresent
3. Just	8. Omnipotent
4. Love	9. Immutable
5. Eternal Life	10. Veracity

Father	Son	Holy Spirit

All these characteristics are found in the Father, Son, and Holy Spirit.

1 *Sovereign.* God has a will. By Himself and with

assistance from no one He makes decisions and policies and sets up principles. He has the right to do as He pleases. He always acts in accordance with all the other attributes of His character, and He will never express one attribute at the expense of another.

For example, a mother may tell a child he will receive a spanking if he plays with matches. But then, when the child plays with the matches and burns himself, she may forgo the spanking and, instead, hold him in her lap and love him. In that case she has expressed her love at the expense of her justice.

Not so with God. He knows how to express His love without compromising His justice (Deuteronomy 4:39; 1 Chronicles 29:12; Psalms 47:2; 83:18; 93:1; 135:6; Daniel 4:35; Acts 17:24).

2 *Righteous.* God is absolute rightness and perfection. It's impossible for Him to do or cause anything that is wrong. He is the standard of all that is right. He is morally perfect without a shadow of deviousness (Ezra 9:15; Psalms 48:10; 119:137; 145:17; Jeremiah 23:6; 1 John 2:29).

3 *Just.* God is absolutely just. It's impossible for Him to do anything that's unfair either to Himself or to man. He executes perfect justice in accordance with His attribute of righteousness. All that is unrighteous must be judged and separated from a relationship with Him (see Romans 1:18; Deuteronomy 32:4; Isaiah 45:21).

4 *Love.* God is perfect, infinite love. It's given freely and without any consideration to the loveliness or merit of the object. It includes His enemies as well as His friends (Matthew 5:44; John 3:16; 16:27; Romans 5:8; Ephesians 2:4; 1 John 3:1; 4:9, 16).

5 *Eternal Life.* There has never been a time when God did not exist, and there never will be a time when He ceases to exist. He is the unmoved Mover, the ground of all being. His existence has no beginning and no end. He is the answer to the

question men have grappled with since the dawn
of history, "What is the power, the force, the
Person who created everything that exists?" He is
the self-existent fount of both physical and spiritual life (Exodus 15:18; Deuteronomy 32:40;
33:27; Job 36:26; Psalms 9:7; 135:13; Lamenta-
tions 5:19; 1 Timothy 1:17; Revelation 1:8).

6 *Omniscient.* God possesses all the knowledge there
is to have. He always has and always will know
everything that has happened, is happening, or
will happen. Nothing ever takes Him by surprise
(Job 26:6; 31:4; 34:21; Psalm 147:5; Proverbs
15:3; Hebrews 4:13; 1 John 3:20).

7 *Omnipresent.* God is infinitely and everywhere
personally present through all of time and space
(Genesis 28:15; 31:3; Deuteronomy 4:39; 31:6;
Joshua 1:9; Psalm 139:8; Proverbs 15:3; Isaiah
66:1; Jeremiah 23:24; Acts 17:27; Hebrews
13:5).

8 *Omnipotent.* God is all powerful, having more
than enough strength to do the sum total of all
things. A question often asked by skeptics is,
"Could God make a rock so big that He couldn't
lift it?" The answer is, "Yes, He could, but to do
so would be to express the attribute of omnipo-
tence at the expense of omniscience, and He
would never do that." In other words, He would
know better than to do it (Job 42:2; 26:7; Psalm
115:3; Matthew 19:26; Mark 14:36; Luke 1:37;
Hebrews 3:6; Revelation 19:6).

9 *Immutable.* God never changes in His nature or
attributes. Therefore we can believe that when
He says He will do something, He'll do it. There
are more than 7,000 things God has promised to
do for those who belong to Him. He can be
trusted to keep His word (Numbers 23:19; Psalm
33:11; Hebrews 1:12; 13:8).

10 *Veracity.* God is absolute truth. Anything in word
or deed that doesn't conform to what He's revealed in His Word is *not* the truth. To know Him

is to know reality (Deuteronomy 32:4; 2 Samuel 7:28; Psalms 33:4; 146:6; Isaiah 65:16).

The Infinite Gap

There's not a person who's ever lived who could stack his life up against the character of God that we've just looked at and then say, "That's just the kind of person I am."

No, the Bible makes a sober statement about what man is like: "The heart of man is deceitful about all things, and desperately wicked" and "All our righteousnesses are as filthy rags" (Jeremiah 17:9; Isaiah 64:6, KJV).

It isn't very flattering, is it? Isaiah isn't saying that it's just our *bad* habits and deeds that are offensive to God. It's what we would consider our *good* human acts that offend God as well. He describes them as *filthy* because by comparison with God's holy character they fall so far short.

I know this is hard to swallow, especially for people who have always prided themselves on the good things they do for God and their fellowman. But listen to what the Apostle James says: "Whoever keeps the whole law and yet stumbles in *one* point, he has become guilty of all [breaking the whole law]" (James 2:10).

The Apostle Paul says virtually the same thing: "Cursed is every one who does not abide by *all things* written in the book of the Law, to perform them" (Galatians 3:10b).

What is the Law?

The Law of God, which is summarized in the ten commandments and the Sermon on the Mount, expresses the overwhelming purity of God's holy character. All the laws that God has ever given to men tell us what we'd have to be like if we were to try to approach God on the basis of our own merit.

But according to James and Paul, we could keep

every single point of the law and yet stumble in just *one small area* and that would be enough to disqualify us from enjoying fellowship with God for even a moment.

What a commentary on the magnitude of God's holiness.

The reason it's so difficult for us to accept the absoluteness of this concept is because of all the relativistic thinking that predominates our lives. We just can't fathom a holiness that won't bend "just a little" to accommodate our human weaknesses. And none of us can believe that those "little" sins we commit could be so offensive to God.

Statistics Don't Lie!

Of course, once we start trying to decide if one of our sins is a little or a big one, we've got a delicate job on our hands. What we call "little" might not seem that way to God at all.

But suppose that an average person sinned only one "little" sin a day from the age of five, until he was sixty-five years old. By that time he would have on his hands (or should I say "conscience") 21,915 sins.

That means that at least 21,915 times the person fell short of measuring up to the character of God which is the perfect standard that God measures man against.

But, you say, suppose for every sin that man committed he did five good deeds. Wouldn't that offset his sins and balance the scorecard?

Let me answer that with an illustration.

Sink or Swim

The State of Hawaii boasts of one of the most comfortable climates in the entire world. Say that you and I want to take a trip there, but neither of us can afford to go by commercial means. So we decide to swim.

Our plan is to meet at 6:00 A.M. one day and leave from Long Beach, California. Our families come down to the ocean to see us off, someone offers up a prayer for divine guidance (we'll need it!), another man fires a pistol with blanks, and away we go.

By midmorning we're exhausted, and by noon we begin to sink. There is no way we can make it. It is simply beyond human ability. Maybe you go fifteen miles, I go ten, but we still fall hopelessly short of the 2,400-mile distance.

Perhaps the greatest swimmer of our times, Olympic seven-Gold-Medalist Mark Spitz, could get in shape for marathon swimming and go two hundred or three hundred miles, but even he would fail, because the standard, in this case, is all the way to Hawaii.

People tend to compare themselves with each other and see who comes the closest to a given mark. But "closeness" doesn't count with God. Closeness counts in darts, horseshoes, and hand grenades, but not in holiness.

What I'm trying to get across is that there is no possible way to achieve right standing with God by our own human efforts. The standard is too tough! There has to be some divine intervention by which man has supernaturally credited to him God's own righteousness.

The Divine Dilemma

We've seen that a major barrier between God and man is the holy character of God. By man's failing to measure up to that he has incurred the just sentencing of God, the "death penalty" (Romans 1:18).

Our first parents, Adam and Eve, were told by God that there would be the awesome consequence of spiritual death immediately, and physical death eventually, if they disobeyed Him. When they flaunted God's command and broke His divine law, they incurred a DEBT OF SIN with God.

When any law is broken, a "debt to the law" is incurred and justice demands retribution of some kind. So it was that when man broke God's law, the *justice* of God (which is one of His character traits) had to demand full payment from man of the threatened penalty of death. This was tantamount to man's banishment from free access to the intimate presence of his loving Creator.

Now, here was God's dilemma (if there could be such a thing). Whereas the *justice* of God burned in wrath against man for outraging God's holiness, God's *love* equally yearned to find a way to justly forgive him and bring him back into fellowship with Himself.

But how could God express His *love*, His *righteousness*, and His *justice* toward man all at the same time and still require that the justly deserved DEBT OF SIN be paid? There was no greater challenge ever to confront God than how He could remain *just* and yet declare sinners forgiven and righteous. How could God satisfy the requirements of His absolute righteousness which could not allow anyone less than that into His presence?

Justice and love both had to be vindicated. But how could they be when the justifiable demand against rebellious man was to banish him forever from the presence of a holy God?

Can a judge whose son has broken the law do away with the law in order to free his son?

The answer to these questions is the most important information you will ever learn and that's what this book is all about.

Chapter Four

Barrier Number Two: A Debt of Sin

To understand the nature of this DEBT OF SIN, we have to reach back into the practices of the criminal courts of the Roman Empire.

In the days of the great dominion of Rome, it was assumed by Caesar that every Roman citizen owed him perfect allegiance and obedience to his laws. Justice was swift to enforce this assumption, and if any citizen broke any law of the land, he soon found himself standing before the courts or Caesar himself.

Nailed to the Prison Door

If the man were found guilty of breaking the law and sentenced to prison, an itemized list was made of each infraction and its corresponding penalty. This list was, in essence, a record of how the man had failed to live up to the laws of Caesar. It was called a "Certificate of Debt."

When the man was taken to his prison cell, this Certificate of Debt was nailed to his cell door so that anyone passing by could tell that the man had been justly condemned and could also see the limitations of his punishment. For instance, if he were guilty of three crimes and the total time of imprisonment were twenty years, then it would be illegal to keep him there twenty-five years, and all could see that.

When the man had served his time and was released, he would be handed the yellowed, tattered Certificate of Debt with the words "Paid in Full" written across it. He could never again be imprisoned for those crimes as long as he could produce his canceled Certificate of Debt.

But until the sentence was paid, that Certificate of Debt stood between him and freedom. It continued to witness to the fact that the imprisoned man had failed to live according to the laws of Rome and was, in essence, an offense to Caesar.

Mankind's "Certificate of Debt"

As we saw in the last chapter, man owes God perfect obedience to His holy laws as summarized in the Ten Commandments and the Sermon on the Mount. By his failure to live up to this standard of perfection, man has become an offense to the very character of God, and the eternal court of justice has pronounced the death sentence upon man.

A Certificate of Debt was prepared against every person who would ever live, listing his failure to live in thought, word, and deed in accordance with the law of God. This death sentence has become a DEBT OF SIN which has to be paid, either by man or, if possible, someone qualified to take his place (Colossians 2:14).

And this DEBT OF SIN has become another piece of the barrier that separates God and man.

Now, the subject of "sin" isn't too popular. You can tell a person that he's failed to measure up to the holy character of God, and if he's even halfway honest he'll have to agree to that, because that doesn't make him sound too bad.

But somehow people don't like to be told that they're

sinners, even though they know they commit "little" sins all the time. It's all part of the relativistic thinking that's become a part of our society and has helped us rationalize all our actions.

It's Not the Fault of the Environment

One look at the morning newspaper is all we need to confirm the mess that men have made of their lives. We don't have to have a degree in psychology, either, to figure out what makes them do what they do. All we have to do is look inside ourselves and we'll see all kinds of emotions, lusts, drives, and temptations that overpower us from time to time and cause us to do things we know are wrong.

Those actions are what God calls "sins," and they *aren't* caused by our environment. They are caused by our "reaction" to our environment, and that's an *internal* problem which man has.

Listen to how Jesus described man and his sinning: "That which comes *out* of the man is what defiles him. For from *inside,* out of the heart of men comes the evil thoughts and fornications, thefts, murders, adulteries, deeds of coveting, and wickedness, as well as deceit, lust, envy, slander, pride and foolishness. All these evil things proceed from *within* and defile man" (Mark 7:20-23).

These words of Jesus blow most of secular psychology right out of the ballpark because they show that man's wrong actions don't come primarily from *without,* they come from *within.* Misbehavior is not primarily the result of our environment; it's a problem of the heart.

The Sin Nature

In using the word "heart," Jesus is talking about that inner part of man's being which has in it the "sin nature," or a disposition toward rebellion against God.

Have you ever done something which was totally stupid and senseless and you said to yourself afterwards, "What on earth made me do that?" Your better judgment *knew* it was wrong, but you went ahead anyway. Well, it was your "sin nature" which prompted you to do it.

The Bible uses the terms "flesh" and "sin" (in the singular) to describe that force within us that is in total rebellion against God. This "nature" was not in man when God created him. It entered Adam and Eve the moment they disobeyed God and He withdrew His spiritual life from them.

Stranger Than Fiction

I saw a science-fiction movie once that made me think of how the sin nature works in us. Men from outer space landed on earth and captured a number of people. They implanted tiny electrodes in the back of their heads through which they could completely control the actions of their victims.

After the spaceships left the earth, their victims remained here and from all appearances seemed to be just like they'd always been. However, anytime the spacemen wanted them to kill someone or follow any other command, they simply transmitted this to their victims, who were forced to obey.

Our sin natures work a lot like that. Satan, either directly or through some subtle temptation that appeals to one of our senses, gets our sin nature to start rebelling against the known will of God for us (as expressed in His laws) and the first thing you know, we've given in to it and sinned.[1]

Do We Sin Because We're Sinners?

Sooner or later most of us get around to wondering, "Do I sin because I'm a sinner, or am I a sinner because I sin?"

---

[1] For a full explanation of how this principle of rebellion to the Law works, see the author's book, *Satan Is Alive and Well on Planet Earth*, chapter 12, "The Guilt Trip" (Grand Rapids: Zondervan Publishing House, 1972).

Now that isn't a silly question like "Which came first, the chicken or the egg?" It's very important to know whether my sinning stems from a nature that I'm born with or whether it's just something I start doing because everyone else does it and it's "catching," like some disease.

The Bible teaches that when Adam and Eve disobeyed God in the Garden of Eden, they didn't just lose their sense of fellowship with God and become unlike Him in their character; they actually had something *added* to them—a sin nature. And that made them sinners. Since that awful day of infamy, all men have been born with that same sinful nature, and that is the source of our sins.

I know it's hard to believe that a tiny, innocent baby cooing sweetly in our arms has in it a sin nature that will soon begin committing sins, but that's what the Bible teaches from start to finish.

When is Sin, Sin?

Is it a sin to be tempted?

The answer to that is No. If a girl in a short miniskirt stoops down to pick a flower and I'm standing right behind her, there's no way I can stop a tempting thought from passing through my mind. But if I continue to look and start to toy with the idea of getting into the sack with her, then it becomes a sin.

The sin is not the temptation; the sin is in not saying No to the temptation and in not handing the matter over to Christ for Him to deal with on the spot.

It's What's Inside That Counts

To me, the greatest thing that true Christianity has to offer the world in general and individuals specifically is that God will go to work on the *inside* and clean us up and make us brand-new people. He'll give a new motivation, new hope, and new power for living. Most religions simply offer an external program or code of ethics that seeks to change a man's outer behavior.

That would be all right if that was where the problem is, but it's not. This sort of outer renovation usually blinds men to the real problem which is on the inside.

I heard once of a girl who was having terrible stomach pains and went to the doctor for some medicine. He gave her a bottle of green-colored liquid and told her to take two tablespoons internally every three hours. Well, she took one whiff of the medicine and nearly vomited. So she hit upon another plan. She decided to *rub* the two tablespoons *on* her stomach every three hours.

The medicine smelled as bad as it looked and strangely enough, although she was saturated with the medicine, she didn't get any better. Of course, when she went back to the doctor, he quickly convinced her that all the medicine in the world rubbed on the *outside* of her stomach wasn't going to get her well. The problem was on the *inside* and that's where the remedy needed to get.

Now, you know, of course, that was only a silly story, but I hope you got the point. The problem that men have is called "sin," and it's down *inside* us. No amount of "medicine" applied to the outside can ever soak through to where this problem of sin is.

Because men can't stand to admit that they have this *internal* weakness called sin, they've invented "religion" and "philosophy." Both these studies more or less admit that mankind has a problem, but generally speaking, they believe it's external in nature and can be solved through rituals or reason.

I personally believe it's another case of the old "ointment on the stomach" routine, and although for many a "patient" the operation appears to be successful, unfortunately the patient dies.

Summing it Up

In summarizing this barrier to God, man's DEBT OF SIN, we can see that man's problem is really twofold.

First is the fact that when Adam and Eve sinned,

they lost their relationship and fellowship with God, and a nature of sin and rebellion against God was introduced into them and through them into all their descendants. This nature is the source of all of our "acts" of sin and is a major reason why we are unacceptable for a relationship with God.

Secondly, a DEBT OF SIN was incurred by them and all mankind which must be paid. The penalty for that debt is death, and it must be paid either by us or by someone qualified to take our place.

Adam Wasn't the Only Culprit

It makes a lot of people angry to hear that something which some far-off ancestor did implicates them with such grievous consequences. And I can sympathize with how they feel.

But in God's mind, Adam was representative man—the federal head of the human race. What he did judicially implicated all his fellowmen. If the President of the United States and our Congress declared war on some country today, I would be at war too, even though I might not personally be in favor of it. It makes no difference whether I voted for them or not. What they did would implicate me because they act as my federal head.

A story I have heard illustrates this very well.

In the days of slavery, old Mose grew weary of working out in the cotton fields and chopping wood day after day and year after year. One day Mose got to thinkin' about whose fault it was that his lot in life was so tough. After finding legitimate excuses for everyone he could think of, he finally decided it was all really Adam's fault for eating that apple in the first place. That drove man out of his lush, comfortable garden home and into the fields to toil by the sweat of his brow.

The more he thought about this, the angrier Mose got with Adam. As he swung his axe into each block of wood, he'd mutter, "Old Adam, old Adam," whacking a little harder with each utterance.

One day his master came along and overheard this tirade. He went up to Mose and asked him what he meant by "Old Adam."

"Well," said Mose, "if it hadn't been for Adam, I wouldn't be stuck out here in this woodpile, slavin' away all day long. I'd be in the house restin' and sippin' lemonade."

The master thought for a minute and then he said to Mose, "You come into the house, Mose. From now on you don't have to do any more hard work. You can lay around all day long, doing whatever you like. There is just one thing, though. See the little box here on the table? I don't want you to open it. Okay? Enjoy yourself now."

Well, for the next few weeks Mose couldn't get over his good fortune. He wandered around the house enjoying his leisure and lemonade.

Then he noticed the box the master had spoken about. At first all he did was look at it. But as the days went by, the temptation grew stronger and stronger to touch it. After a few days of only feeling it and carrying it around, it finally got too much for him and he couldn't imagine what harm there'd be in just a little peek into it.

As he cautiously opened one corner of it, a white piece of paper inside caught his eye. His curiosity wouldn't be satisfied until he'd taken out the paper and read it. This is what it said:

"Mose, you old rascal. I don't ever want you blaming Adam anymore. If you'd been there in the garden, you'd have done the same thing Adam did. Now, you hightail it back out to the woodpile and get to chopping again."

The point of the story is evident. If we'd been in Adam's shoes, the chances are very good we'd have done the same thing he did. God in His great foreknowledge (His omniscience) could see that all men would, indeed, ratify Adam's rebellion in their own behavior.

If God had left it there and never done anything to

reconcile man to Himself, then He might be considered unfair.

But the good news of the "Gospel" is that God so loved the world that, at infinite cost to Himself, He provided a means of removing man's DEBT OF SIN and of dealing with the nature of sin in men.

CHARACTER
OF GOD

DEBT OF SIN

SLAVERY
TO SATAN

Chapter Five
Barrier Number Three: Slavery To Satan

Up to now we have dealt with two of the basic problems that help form the barrier that exists between God and man. We've seen how man's sin was an affront to the holy CHARACTER OF GOD, and how his failure to keep God's laws resulted in a DEBT OF SIN.

Now let's take a look at the third barrier separating God and man, the fact that man is in SLAVERY TO SATAN.

I know this assertion will raise bristles with many people because Jesus got the same reaction when He told some of *His* generation that Satan was their father.

The Truth is Often Unpopular

During the early part of His ministry Jesus got into frequent hassles with some of His fellow Jews. On one occasion He was talking with a group of militant Jews who maintained that because they were born of the stock of Abraham, they were "in," and that they had it made with God as their Father.

Jesus told them that if God were their Father, they would have loved Him (Jesus) for He had come from the Father and had in fact been sent by Him to the earth.

"Why don't you understand what I'm saying?" He queried.

And then answering His own question, He said with an air of authority, "It is because you cannot hear My word. You are of your *father* the devil, and you want to do the desires of your father. He was a murderer from the beginning, and does not stand in the truth, because there is no truth in him. Whenever he speaks a lie, he speaks from his own nature; for he is a liar, and the father of lies" (John 8:43, 44).

Needless to say, the reaction Jesus got to this scathing indictment wasn't too favorable. In fact, after calling Him the two dirtiest names they could think of —*Samaritan* (a hated half-breed Jew) and *demon-possessed*—they eventually tried to stone Him, but He slipped out of their hands.

The Two "Fatherhoods" of Mankind

What were the grounds Jesus had for telling His fellow Jews that they were children of Satan?

There were two prime factors.

First, the Jews prided themselves on being children of Abraham by physical descent and therefore children of God as a result. Jesus didn't dispute their claim to physical relationship with Abraham, but He emphatically denied that it made them children of *God*. He told them that unless they had the same faith in Him, as Messiah, which Abraham had had, then Abraham's God wasn't their father, Satan was.

The second point Jesus sought to hammer home was that there are only *two* fatherhoods of mankind, the fatherhood of God and the fatherhood of Satan. So, if they weren't God's children, then they must have been Satan's.

That statement made the Jews furious, and it still affects people that way today. But there's a reason why there's such a violent reaction to this truth. It's because one of Satan's chief tactics down through the history of mankind has been to blur and confuse people on this very issue. It makes it much easier for him to maintain control over his "children" if they don't fully comprehend who their father really is.

How successful Satan has been in this area is evidenced by the number of churches of all religions, including Christianity, which have as a basic tenet of their religion that God is the father of all mankind and therefore we're all brothers.

As admirable as it is to want to practice brotherhood, and without my impugning the need for it, the truth of the matter is that God is the *creator* of all men, but only the *father* of those who have His *spiritual life* in them.

When man was created, he *did* have God's spiritual life resident within him, but when he sinned and turned his back on God, he lost that spiritual life. Now every man is born without it, and if he wants God to be his father for now and through eternity, he must have God's life put back into him sometime before he dies physically on this earth.

A Powerful Adversary

How did Satan get to be the powerful authority he seems to be? That he does have power, there is no doubt. History is strewn with the wreckage he's made of individuals and nations.

A classic example of the evil that just one man could do when brought under Satan's *direct* control is the story of Adolf Hitler. There is ample evidence that he was either demon-possessed or possessed by Satan himself.

But damage as great as that is caused every day in this world by a system of thinking and acting which is subtly controlled by Satan to exclude the need for God. The toll in human suffering, physically, emotionally, and spiritually from a lack of a true relationship with God, is incalculable. Broken homes, suicides, murders, rape, greed, hate—all these and more are mute testimony to the fact that this world couldn't possibly be the way God had originally planned for it to be.

Adam's Power-of-Attorney

In the Book of Genesis we're told that God put man on earth and entrusted him with authority over himself and all of God's creation. Man was told by God to be fruitful and multiply and replenish, subdue, and have dominion over every living thing that moved on the earth (Genesis 1:28).

In other words, God put man in charge of this planet and its inhabitants. And aside from the one restraint that God gave them, not to eat of the Tree of the Knowledge of Good and Evil, no other stipulations were laid down as to how they were to govern God's creation.

I'm sure that's because Adam was a loved and trusted friend of God. And on this basis God gave him the power-of-attorney to govern this planet in God's stead.

A Wolf in Snake's Clothing!

But there was another personage already there in the garden with Adam when God put him in charge. That person was one who had already made known to God and all His angelic hosts that he wanted to usurp the place of Number One from his creator God.[1]

The name of this being was Lucifer (later known as Satan or the Devil). He was power mad! More than anything else he wanted to control what God had created.

So there he was in the garden. And through his subtle lies and innuendos about God, he convinced Adam and Eve that God was holding out on them by not wanting them to eat of that tree. He told them that

---

[1] For a fuller understanding of Satan, his origin, and his fall, read the author's book, *Satan Is Alive and Well on Planet Earth* (Grand Rapids: Zondervan Publishing House, 1972).

God didn't want to share His power with them and that since that tree would make them as wise as God, that's why He had forbidden them to eat of it.

We look back at that scene now and see the paradise they were enjoying. Then we look at the mess the world is in today and we say, "Wow! They didn't know how good they had it. How on earth could they have blown it so badly and felt that God was holding out on them when they'd already been given such fantastic power and authority?"

Mankind's Benedict Arnold!

If only Adam and Eve had realized the devastating consequences that would result from their disobedience to God's one prohibition.

Not only did they lose their spiritual life and ability to have free access into the presence and fellowship of God, but in capitulating to Satan's temptation they unwittingly turned over their God-given power and authority to Satan's control. He became the legal controller of all men who would ever be born from Adam's seed. He also took control of the planet itself and all creation on it, animal and vegetable.

"But," you may be saying, "how could God permit such a terrible thing to happen? Couldn't He have taken the power away from Satan once he'd gotten it from Adam?"

No, He couldn't. You see, God is so just in His nature that He couldn't even be unjust to Satan. A legal transference of property and power had taken place, and a legal means of reversing it would have to be found.

The Slave Market of Sin

This sellout of Adam to Satan is how the world got into the mess it's in today. With Satan as the legal ruler of this planet, it become one great big slave market and everyone born into it of Adam's seed is born a slave of Satan.

This was clearly taught by Jesus and His disciples.

The Apostle John wrote, "The whole world lies in the power of the evil one" (1 John 5:19b). The word "world" in that verse is the Greek word, *cosmos,* which means an orderly system. This is what is meant when we say that Satan calls the shots over this present world system.

The great defender of the faith, Paul, called Satan "the god of this world" and said he had "blinded the minds of the unbelieving, that they might not see the light of the gospel of the glory of Christ, who is the image of God" (2 Corinthians 4:4).

In another place in the New Testament Paul spoke of Satan as "the prince of the power of the air" and called him "the spirit that is now working in the sons of disobedience" (Ephesians 2:1-4).

When the Apostle Paul stood on trial before the great King Agrippa to defend the message he had been preaching, he clearly declared man's need of being set free from SLAVERY TO SATAN when he said, "[Jesus sent me] to open their eyes so that they may turn from darkness to light and *from the dominion of Satan to God*" (Acts 26:18).

Jesus' Temptations

The most arrogant display of Satan's authority is seen in his attempt to get Jesus to sin.

You see, Jesus is the only person ever born into this world who was not born under Satan's dominion. The reason is that Jesus did not have a human father, and therefore the curse of SLAVERY TO SATAN which was passed from Adam to all his descendants didn't affect Him.

Jesus was called the "second Adam" because He was the second man who was brought into this world perfect (1 Corinthians 15:4-5). He could have sinned, just as the first Adam had done, but had He done so He would have been brought under Satan's dominion, just as Adam had been.

Because He was the only person ever born into this

world who wasn't a slave to Satan, He became the special object of Satan's hatred. He sought continually either to kill Jesus before He could go to the cross, or to get Him to sin so He would be brought under Satan's authority as all unredeemed sinners are.

That's why on one occasion when Satan was tempting Jesus, he showed Him all the kingdoms of the world and their glory and then he said to Him, "I will give you all this domain and its glory; for it has been handed over to me, and I can give it to whomever I wish. Therefore if You worship before me it shall all be Yours" (Luke 4:6, 7).

No Crown Without a Cross

Jesus didn't dispute Satan's claim for a moment. He knew that the world and mankind had been legally transferred by Adam into Satan's control. He also knew He could take it back from Satan anytime He chose to. But had He done so, it would have meant bypassing the cross because it was there God intended that the ransom price be paid to free enslaved mankind and restore the rightful rulership of the world to God.

For Him to have chosen the easy way and taken the crown of dominion from Satan when He offered it would have been sin. And the minute He had sinned, He, too, would have entered into the slave market of sin and come under Satan's control.

Consequently there would have been no "free man" in the world who would pay the ransom price and set men free from their bondage to Satan. All would have been in the slave market together, and none could have qualified to buy anyone else's freedom.

Satan is "Some" Father!

At the beginning of this chapter we talked about a conversation Jesus had with some unbelieving Jews and how He had told them that Satan was their father.

When you think of someone as being a "father," you usually picture some kindly, concerned, and tenderhearted person who has his children's best interests at heart.

But, though Satan knows how to masquerade as an "angel of light," his heart is black and evil, full of hate and bitter revenge against God and men. This is no normal father. This is an evil, sadistic creature who has imprisoned his children in a slave camp, caring nothing for them as human beings. He uses them for his purposes and then throws them on a junk heap when he's finished with them.

His only worry is that someday they might find out that a ransom has been paid for their freedom and there is no longer any reason for them to be held in bondage.

But until they find this out, man's SLAVERY TO SATAN is a barrier to a restored fellowship with God, the heavenly Father.

CHARACTER OF GOD

DEBT OF SIN

SLAVERY TO SATAN

SPIRITUAL DEATH

Chapter Six

Barrier Number Four: Spiritual Death

A friend told me a story once that's a pretty clear illustration of what it's like to be spiritually dead.

He said his son had gotten an electric train for Christmas and together the two of them got it all set up. They spent hours playing with it, and the train raced up and down the tracks through the tunnels and in and out of the depot.

One day when he came home from work, his son met him at the door and was really upset: the train wouldn't run. Together they took the electrical mechanisms apart, but they all checked out fine. They checked the connections between all the cars, and they were all in place.

After hours of trying to get the train running it was just no use. There was no power getting through to the train. For all practical purposes it was dead.

Then, by chance, my friend spotted a small metal crossing sign that had fallen across the tracks and was obscured by some buildings along the rails. As he

picked up the crossing sign from the tracks, the train
began to roll.

What had happened was that the metal on the
tracks had caused a short circuit. All the power of the
City of Los Angeles was kept from entering that train
because of a tiny piece of seemingly insignificant metal.

Mankind is "Short-Circuited"

As we've looked at in previous chapters, there was a
time when God and man experienced an unbroken
fellowship and things were fine between them. Then
something happened that short-circuited the relationship between God and man. Something fell across mankind's "tracks," and all the divine power and spiritual
life of the omnipotent Creator God were cut off from
His special creation, man, and he became dead spiritually.

That "something" was sin!

It's not as though this awful consequence took Adam
and Eve by surprise. God had told them that if they
ate of the Tree of the Knowledge of Good and Evil,
they would die (Genesis 2:17). But since they had
never seen anything die before this, they didn't fully
comprehend what "death" meant.

The Three Faces of Death

Adam and Eve had no idea how utterly disastrous it
would be to be *spiritually dead* in relationship to their
wonderful Creator. Likewise they didn't comprehend
the horror of eventually being cut off from each other
and their loved ones by *physical death*. And finally,
they failed completely to realize the implications of
eternal death, that condition of separation from God for
eternity.

Although all three aspects of this death sentence im-
posed upon them went into effect immediately, only
one was instantly evident to man himself. He knew
that something irreparable had happened to his rapport
with God.

That "something" was *SPIRITUAL DEATH*.

Adam and Eve immediately felt an alienation from God and even went so far as to hide themselves from Him. But even though God went looking for them and, by His gracious words and actions to them, reassured them of His love, He nevertheless had to execute the sentence of death and separate man from fellowship with Himself. Hence Adam was banished from the garden and free access to God.

The "Sin" Infection

Sin and death had entered the human race through one man's disobedience (Romans 5:12). When Adam sinned he *became* a sinner, and that one sin infected the whole human race, still in his loins, with the sickness of sin and death. Since then, all men are *born* sinners with the sentence of death upon them.

A Look at Man From God's Viewpoint

There's no way even to begin to understand how that event in the garden affected mankind down through the centuries and even today, until we get a look at God as He really is, and ourselves as He sees us.

In creating man, God anticipated every physical and mental faculty that man would ever need to relate to the beautiful material world into which He placed him.

However, God also equipped man to function in relation to the nonphysical or spiritual realm which was also a reality. He did so by giving man a soul and spirit.

The following diagram gives you a picture of how the three parts of man's make-up work together. When seeking to express divine truth, no human illustration is perfect, but this diagram suffices to give us the framework we need for looking at the interwoven and sometimes separate functions of the body, soul, and spirit of man.

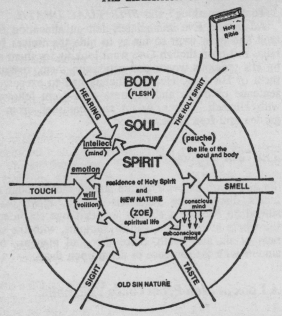

BORN AGAIN BELIEVER

The Body

The body is the *material* part of man, that part which enables him to function in and relate to the physical world around him. The body contains physical life. This is an illusive, indefinable force which keeps the heart beating. Despite the various efforts to create human life in test tubes, no one has succeeded in creating and sustaining the kind of life necessary to cause a human body to function as designed.

When the body dies, it returns to the dust it was taken from. But that's not the end of it. Eventually it will be brought back together again and have an eternal existence, either with God or separated from Him.

The Soul

The soul is the immaterial part of man. When God formed man, He breathed into man's nostrils the breath of *lives* and man became a living soul (Genesis 2:7). The Hebrew word translated "life" in most English versions of the Bible should actually have been translated "lives" because it's a plural word in the original Hebrew Bible.

I believe it was no accident that the Bible says God breathed into man "lives" instead of "life," because all through the rest of the Bible two kinds of life are spoken of in relation to man—soulish life and spiritual life.

The soulish life contains the image of God in man. Being in the image of God means that man, like God, has intellect, emotion, moral reasoning, volition, and eternity of being. It does not refer to us "looking" like God physically, however, or having His *spiritual* life in us.

Physical life and soulish life are one and the same. For, if you take the physical life from a man, his soul also departs from his body. And if you take the soul of a man, it means he is dead physically. Even though a person may live for many years in a state of deep unconsciousness, it doesn't mean his soul has left him. It's simply that his physical body will not respond to the impulses sent to it from his soul.

The five senses located in the physical body are the windows of the soul. They're the means of bringing the information about the physical world into the mind of man. But their limitation is that they can't substantiate any reality which is outside their scope, the material world.

For instance, the rationality that much of the world has is that if it can't be seen, tasted, touched, smelled, or heard, it isn't real. This approach to life is usually called "materialistic" or "empiricist." The problem with this philosophy is that it shuts out a whole realm of existence that's outside the world of the senses.

This is the realm of the spirit.

The Spirit

When God breathed into man the breath of lives, not only did He give him soulish or physical life, but He also gave man God's own kind of life—spiritual life.

You see, God is spirit and in order to worship Him the way He has ordained or fellowship with Him on a personal basis, we must also be spiritual creatures (John 4:24).

That's why God created man with a human spirit. It was to be the part of man to contain God's life, spiritual life. Adam and Eve had soulish life *and* spiritual life. With their soulish life they comprehended the beauty of their physical surroundings and each other. With their spiritual life they experienced communication with God who was present in the garden as a spirit.

You might say that man was originally created with *six* senses instead of five. Five of them plugged him in to the physical world and operated on *soulish* power, but the sixth sense, which is called "faith," operated on *spiritual* power. It enabled him to establish reality in the spiritual realm and experience uninhibited communication with God.

The Tragedy of The Fall

Aside from all the other disastrous consequences of man's disobedience to God, perhaps the worst is that God withdrew from man His spiritual life and left man with a dead spirit, a spiritual vacuum if you please. No longer did man have the internal spiritual equipment to experience a relationship with God who is a spirit. Within a few generations of Adam, men had so lost their concept of the one true God that they wandered hopelessly in spiritual darkness.

You can see the dilemma that arose between God and man. Whereas God had made man in such a way that it would be possible for communication with him through his spirit, now that man no longer had spiritual life, God had to communicate with men in ways that their five senses could comprehend.

That's the whole story of the Bible: God seeking ways to make fallen man aware of His existence, His love, and His judgment against sin. But always God had to take the initiative and reach out to man in ways that he could understand by sight, hearing, taste, touch, or smell.

The Barrier is Complete

So here we have the complete picture of the universal barrier which separates man from God. Man can't tear the barrier down and he can't climb over it by his own efforts. In fact, he can't even climb over with God's help. The barrier must come down, and God alone can do that.

You will meet people every day who say they have no need for God and don't feel any of the barriers we've looked at. But the crucial issue is that God says they have a need whether they are aware of that need or not. And His Word shows very clearly what the need is.

I may visit the doctor, and he could say to me, "Hal, you have a severe illness which proper treatment can completely cure."

"But, Doc, I don't *feel* sick."

"No matter. Tests show conclusively that you're ill."

Since he's an expert in his field, I really have little choice but to take his word for it. After all, effective cure depends completely on accurate diagnosis. But after the diagnosis is made, I've got to submit myself to the cure.

God says we have a problem. That problem is called sin. It's a fatal disease with only one known cure. Let's take a look now at what that remedy is.

Chapter Seven

Why God Had To Become Man

Have you ever stopped to wonder what the main factor is that divides true Christianity and most other religions?

Christians accept the same God of the Old Testament that Jews and several other religions do. But where they part company with other creeds is in the Christian teaching that the God of the Old Testament actually put on a human body for thirty-three years, and without ceasing to be God, He lived on this earth as a man.

To many religions, and Jews especially, this concept is blasphemy. But in true Christianity, this conviction that God took on human form is so central that unless it's true, there is no adequate explanation as to how the barriers that separate God and man could be torn down.

Furthermore, Christians believe that the Old Testament gave ample testimony to the fact that God would one day take on humanity in His plan to redeem man-

kind and bring about a reconciliation between God
and man.

But before we look at who this God-man might be,
let's see why it would have been necessary for God to
have become a man.

The Communication Problem

We're very conscious of this problem in our modern
world. Marriage counselors tell us that the failure to
communicate is one of the main factors in couples not
being able to reconcile differences. Parents and children grow apart because of this problem.

But as bad as these communication failures are, the
worst breakdown that man has in this area is between
himself and God.

We've already seen why this is. It's because God is a
spirit and can be understood in the deepest sense only
by one who also has spiritual life. Men are born with
soulish life which gives them a world-consciousness,
but they lack spiritual life whereby they can communicate with God.

Therefore, since the fall of man, God has had to
take into account man's inability to comprehend spiritual truth by spiritual means. He has been forced to
reveal Himself to men in ways that they could understand with their soulish life and their five senses, but it
was always with a view to bringing them to a point of
submission to Him.

His problem was similar to that of the naturalist who
had a special concern for a certain ant hill which he
had been observing for months. Each day the man
spent hours watching the intricate maneuverings of
these ants and had come to the place where he felt a
very special affinity for them.

One day the naturalist saw a huge bulldozer in the
distance and immediately realized that this ant hill lay
right in the path of the construction of a new road.

The man panicked. He desperately searched his
mind for a way to remove the ants. He scooped up
handfuls of them, but they only bit him. He thought of

building a fence around the ant pile, but realized the bulldozer would only tear it down.

In his frenzied mind he thought to himself, "If only I could speak to them and tell them about the danger ahead of them. If only I could make them see that I'm their friend and only want to save them from destruction."

But despite his great concern, he could think of no way to communicate to them in a way they would understand. To be able to do that, he'd have to become an ant himself, and yet retain the nature of a man so he could continue to clearly assess the problem and make it known to the ants.

God's "Ant Hill," the World!

Down through the long history of the human race, God has spared no effort to reveal Himself to man in terms of natural and material phenomena which man could comprehend.

David, the Psalmist, tells us that the whole world is God's "kindergarten" to teach us the ABCs of the reality of God and the spiritual realm.

The heavens are telling of the glory of God; and the earth is declaring the work of His hands.

Day to Day pours forth speech, and night to night reveals knowledge.

There is no speech, nor are there words; their voice is not heard. Their *sound* has gone out through all the earth, and their utterances to the end of the world (Psalm 19:1-4a).

This is one of the most profound things ever said in the Bible. It tells us that the great majesty and marvel of the universe with its heavenly bodies, and the beauty, the wonder, the incredible balance of design and function of all the creation of God on the earth, are the actual *verbalization* of the fact that God's hands created them.

The fact that day follows day with such certainty

and night after night appears like clockwork is the same as God actually *speaking* to man about His reality and trustworthiness.

David said, "They aren't *actually* speaking nor can you listen intently and hear any words as such, but nevertheless, their *sound* has gone out to all the earth."

Why the Sound?

What's the purpose of this grandiose demonstration in nature of the reality of God?

The Apostle Paul in the New Testament gives us the answer to that question.

"That which is known about God is evident within [men]; for God made it evident to them. For since the creation of the world His invisible attributes, His eternal power and divine nature, have been clearly seen, being understood through what has been made, *so that they are without excuse*" (Romans 1:19, 20).

Paul says the true nature of the invisible God has been openly revealed by His material creation so that the soulish intellects of men could put two and two together and come up with the realization that God exists.

But not only to recognize that He exists. They also are without excuse for not knowing that He will eventually judge ungodliness and the suppression of the truth that He is the sovereign authority over men (Romans 1:18).

Nature's Lesson Ignored

It's fairly obvious to a fair-minded thinker that most people down through the history of mankind did not conclude from nature's lesson that there was only one God and He was knowable and worthy of their praise.

There's no question but what all civilizations had a concept of some supreme force that wasn't completely controllable by them. And there is abundant evidence in archaeology that men had gods and worshiped them.

But the Apostle Paul tells us what the problem was with this. He says that even though men knew from nature that there was a creator God, they didn't honor Him in their own lives as sovereign, but went about their daily lives as though He had no say-so over them.

Then they would sit around and make futile speculations about what He looked like, where He lived, was He married, did He have children, was He kind and benevolent or harsh and cruel, and eventually they ended up making some kind of an image or statue of one of God's creations and worshiped it (see Romans 1:21-25).

You see, since they were men who were spiritually dead, they could not have understood fully what God was like, but they had enough light given to them through nature to reach out to the one true God and submit themselves to Him. Had they done so, He would have imparted spiritual life to their dead human spirits and they could have become children of God. Acts 17:26, 27 says that if men had even so much as "blindly groped" for God, they would have found Him.

Into the Arena of Humanity

As powerful as God's nature lesson has been, it was never intended as God's ultimate revelation of Himself to man. The only way for a spirit God to really be able to do and say what He wanted to, was to actually leave His eternal residence and enter the arena of humanity.

Even then He wouldn't be able to communicate with man who is strictly a physical creature unless He, God, also took on physical form and life. It would also be necessary for Him to retain His divine nature and intellect, or He wouldn't be able to accomplish what He'd come to earth to say and do.

The Barriers Have to Go!

But what was the *main* necessity for God to come to earth?

It was to tear down the barriers that man had erected between himself and God. No one but God Himself was capable of doing that job. Man couldn't eradicate the obstacles that separated him from God because of the consequences of sin which crippled him spiritually and made him unacceptable to God.

Some have felt that God could have stayed in heaven but directed men as to how to remove the barriers. This is the "God helps those who help themselves" philosophy. Unfortunately none of man's efforts alone or with God will work because in neither case is any provision made to remove sin which caused the barrier in the first place. Also it would leave man's sentence of death unpaid, and the justice of God would be compromised.

No! For a holy God who had an unquenchable love for man and a divine necessity to vindicate His justice, the only solution was to leave the glory of heaven, take on flesh and blood, and enter the human race. Since He is the supreme sovereign of the universe, this in no way tainted His deity. God could take on any form He wanted to, and it wouldn't have affected who He intrinsically was.

God's Provision For Forgiveness

You'll remember that in the account of the temptation of Adam and Eve, after they had sewn fig leaves together in an effort to hide their shame of transgression from God, God rejected that clothing and took the skins of some animals and clothed them. If you think about it for a minute, you'll realize that the death of those animals is the first record of any creature dying physically.

The animals themselves had done nothing worthy of death, but in their dying a pattern was established by God—an innocent substitute of God's choosing had to shed its blood and thereby provide a *temporary* forgiveness and covering for man's sin.

Several hundred years later when God's law was given through Moses, He instructed him to write, "Without the shedding of blood there is no remission of sin" (Hebrews 9:22 paraphrased).

That was the basis of the whole Jewish system of animal sacrifice—an innocent substitute could bear the sin and death penalty due man if the sacrifice were offered to God in accordance with His ordained system of sacrifice and with expectant faith in His forgiveness.

But Why Become a Man?

The animal sacrifice system couldn't go on forever because it provided only a temporary covering of man's sin from God's eyes.

The New Testament writer of the letter to the Hebrews said, "It is impossible for the blood of bulls and goats to take away sins." And then he added, "Every priest stands daily ministering and offering time after time the same sacrifices, which can never take away sins" (Hebrews 10:4, 11). You see, animal sacrifice never took sins away; it merely covered them temporarily from God's judgment.

The whole picture God wanted people to understand from the animal sacrifices was that God's justice demanded that someone had to take the penalty of death which was due man because of his sin. The fact that God would not exact the penalty from man and would allow a substitute to die in man's place was designed to show man the depths of God's love.

But God never planned that His forgiveness would go on being temporary and conditional. From the moment of man's fall in the garden God had in mind a plan that would provide a *permanent* forgiveness of sin and removal of the barriers separating God and man.

God's Plan For a Man

Since it was human beings who had sinned and incurred the penalty of spiritual and physical death, another true human being would have to be God's final and permanent substitute for man. It would have to be someone of God's choosing who could qualify to step in as a substitute and take the compounded wrath of God against *all sin* that would ever be committed. The covering for sin provided by the animal sacrifices never included *all* the sins of a man. And, of course, it made no provision for men who didn't participate in this ritual.

But in order for a man to qualify to take man's place of judgment and be his sin-bearer, there are five things that would have to be true of him:

1. He would have to be a true human being, born into this world the same way other men are. He would have to live and die in the same manner all humans do.

2. He would have to be without any personal sin of his own for which he would already be under God's condemnation. He would have to be born without a sin nature just as Adam was created without one. At no time in his life could he have ever committed even one sin, and yet, he would have to be subjected to real temptations just as Adam had been.

3. He would have to live under God's law and keep it perfectly. He would have to be absolutely righteous in his nature and in all actions so that God's holy character would be satisfied that here was a man who never broke God's law even once in motive, act, or word.

4. He would have to have full knowledge of what he was doing.

5. He would have to be willing to take mankind's guilt and be judged and put to death for that guilt in the place of and for the sake of mankind.

What a Man!

The whole reason for the writing of this book is to set forth the fact that just such a person came into the world, according to promise, nineteen hundred years ago. He perfectly fulfilled each qualification to be the Savior of men.

That man was called Jesus Christ.

Chapter Eight

The Man that God Became

One of the things that has made the Old Testament scriptures so enduring and always relevant is its prophetic emphasis. Not only was history accurately recorded for us, but hundreds of predictions of future things were made.

Many of these had to do with the appearance in Israel of a great personage who was prophesied to bring a kingdom of peace on earth and rule it with righteousness and justice.

This man was referred to as the "Messiah."

There were perhaps hundreds of zealous reformers who appeared on the pages of Israel's history seeking to fulfill the messianic commission of establishing a kingdom of God on earth. Most of them passed from the scene with little notice or remembrance.

But one man didn't!

It can be clearly demonstrated that nearly three hundred of the prophecies about the Messiah actually found a literal fulfillment in the birth, life, and death

71

of Jesus of Nazareth. The chances of this happening
by mere coincidence are mathematically of such magnitude that it's impossible to calculate.

The Witness of Prophecy

As you put together the pieces of prophecy in the Old
Testament concerning the Messiah, it becomes clear
that in some way this promised Messiah would be both
God and man. This is evident from the number of
times the prophecies referred to Him as a "child" or
"son" who would be born. Then, often in the same
context it spoke of Him as being eternal and God.

Let's look at some of these well-known Old Testament prophecies.

Isaiah 7:14 says, "Therefore the Lord Himself will
give you a sign: Behold, a virgin will be with child and
bear a son, and she will call His name Immanuel." The
word "Immanuel" in Hebrew means "God with us."

I'm aware of the efforts of some Bible interpreters to
dismiss this as a prophecy that found its fulfillment in
Jesus' virgin birth. They point out that the Hebrew
word *alma* used for "virgin" can also be translated
"young woman."

It's true that it can be. But the biggest textual argument *against* translating it as "young woman" is that
at least 160 years before Jesus was born, a translation
of the Old Testament was made into Greek and the
brilliant Hebrew scholars who made that translation,
which is called "The Septuagint," translated the Hebrew word *alma* into the Greek word *parthenos*. And
that Greek word can *only* mean "virgin."

So, many years before Jesus was born, it was clearly
understood that a virgin would bear a son whose name
would mean "God is with us."

In another part of the Book of Isaiah, he writes,
"For a child will be born to us, a son will be given to
us; and the government will rest on His shoulders; and
His name will be Wonderful Counselor, *Mighty God,
Eternal Father,* Prince of Peace.

"There will be no end to the increase of His government or of peace, on the throne of David and over his kingdom, to establish it and to uphold it with justice and righteousness from then on and *forevermore*" (Isaiah 9:6, 7).

Isaiah spoke here of one who would sit on the throne of David forever. He called him the "Mighty God" and the "Eternal Father."

In using these names, there can be no question but that he was speaking of the God of Israel who would one day assume a human body and allow Himself to be brought into this world like any other man, through the means of a human birth.

Micah the prophet, seven hundred years before Jesus was born, prophesied that the Messiah would be born in a small town in Judah called Bethlehem. He said of this town, "From you One will go forth for Me to be ruler in Israel. His goings forth are from long ago, from the *days of eternity*" (Micah 5:2).

There's no doubt that this prophecy was understood to be concerning the promised Messiah, because at the time of Jesus' birth when the wise men came from the East with their gifts, they asked the religious leaders of the nation of Israel where their Messiah-king would be born. The Jewish priests consulted their scriptures, found the prophecy of Micah 5:2, and then sent the wise men down to Bethlehem.

If the priests had only been "wise men," they would have gone to worship their Messiah too!

The Son of God

Any honest investigation of these and the hundreds of other prophecies concerning Messiah will bring you to the conclusion that no one but Jesus of Nazareth could have fulfilled them.

Jesus was called by many names. The name "Christ" was the Greek word for "Messiah." "Jesus of Nazareth" denoted His hometown. He loved to be called "the Son of Man" because it reminded Him of His kinship with humanity whom He loved so dearly.

But I suspect His favorite name was "the Son of

God" because it let the whole world know who His Father was.

The angel in announcing the conception of Jesus to Mary said, "And behold, you will conceive in your womb, and bear a son and you shall name Him Jesus. . . . The Holy Spirit will come upon you and the power of the Most High will overshadow you; and for that reason *the holy offspring* shall be called the Son of God" (Luke 1:31, 35).

The "Most High" who overpowered Mary was none other than God Himself. In some miraculous way, the ovum in the womb of Mary was impregnated with life apart from a human father. God simply put the spark of life into it, and one by one the cells began to divide and multiply and in nine months the baby Jesus was born.

God was the father of the *humanity* of Jesus. The deity of Jesus is not the focus of the title "Son of God," for His divinity needed no father. He's called the Son of God because in His *human* nature He *is* the Son of God. It's so simple it's profound.

Hypostatic Union

This big phrase, "hypostatic union," is a theological term which describes the twofold nature of Jesus. Here's what it means: In the one Person of Jesus Christ there were two natures—*undiminished deity* and *true humanity*. These two natures are never confused in essence or function, and Jesus will have this double nature from the day He assumed it in the manger in Bethlehem, throughout all eternity.

I mention the hypostatic union because it's often the key to understanding why He said what He did in the gospels. He sometimes spoke with reference to His deity as when He said, "I and the Father are one [essence]" (John 10:30). But most of the time He spoke from His humanity, "If you loved Me, you would have rejoiced, because I go to the Father; for the Father is greater than I" (John 14:28).

In Jesus' humanity, He is subject to the Father because the Father is greater than His humanity. But in His deity, He is coequal with God the Father because He is of one essence with Him.

Out of Eternity into Time

Jesus Christ who, as God, always existed in the Godhead with the Father and the Holy Spirit, some two thousand years ago left the Throne of God to come to earth and become a man. Considering the repugnance that this must have meant for One who had never known anything but the sinlessness of heaven, we should consider carefully why He did it.

Let's enumerate seven reasons why God found it necessary to take on visible form and become the man Jesus Christ.

1. *God became a man in order to be the Savior of men.* In writing about the origin of Jesus, the Apostle John calls Him a unique name, "the Word." He says the Word existed before the beginning of all things. He was there face to face with God and was, in fact, God (John 1:1).

Then John says, "And the Word became flesh, and dwelt among us, and we beheld His glory, glory as of the only begotten from the Father, full of grace and truth" (John 1:14).

There's no possible way to misunderstand what John is saying. You may disagree with it, but his statement is clear. This One, called the Word, who was present in the beginning of time and who was God, took on flesh and dwelt down here on earth among men.

Why do you suppose Jesus was called "the Word"? It's because He was the personification of all that the Father wanted to *say* to men.

Two Conditions Contrasted

On several occasions in the New Testament, Jesus is referred to as "the second Adam." It's because as a man He perfectly fulfilled all the dreams and aspirations that God had originally had for the first Adam.

The two conditions of mankind are often contrasted by what Adam brought down on man and what Jesus did to reverse it. Let's look at several of these contrasts.

"For since by a man [*Adam*] came death, by a man [*Jesus*] also came the resurrection of the dead. For as in Adam all die, so also in Christ all shall be made alive" (1 Corinthians 15:21,22).

"For if by the transgression of the one [*Adam*], death reigned through the one, much more those who receive the abundance of grace and of the gift of righteousness will reign in life through the One, Jesus Christ.

"So then as through one transgression [*Adam's*] there resulted condemnation to all men; even so through one act of righteousness [*Christ's* death] there resulted justification of life to all men.

"For as through the one man's disobedience [*Adam's*] the many [*mankind*] were made sinners, even so through the obedience of the One [*Jesus*] the many will be made righteous" (Romans 5:17-19).

The point of all these verses is that the first man got mankind into all its trouble, but God sent another Man into the world and He undid it.

In order to qualify as a true human being who could undo sin's damage, Jesus did not use His divine power while He was on earth. Paul tells us that "although He existed in the form of God, [He] did not regard equality with God a thing to be clung to, but He laid aside His divine privileges, taking the form of a bond-servant, and being made in the likeness of men" (Philippians 2:6,7 paraphrased).

Jesus' whole life was lived in total dependence upon the Father who worked through Him by the Holy Spirit who indwelt Him. That's the exact way that God intended for all men to live. If Jesus had ever withstood one temptation or performed one miracle using His own divine power, He would not have been behaving as a true man and He would have disqualified Himself from being the Savior of men. (See John 5:19,30.)

Now, let's look at another reason why God had to become man.

2. *He had to be someone who could and would die for men.*

What is sin's penalty? Death. Can God die? Obviously not. Therefore the One who would take the penalty for man had to be a true human being as well as truly God.

The writer of Hebrews said that by the grace of God, Jesus came so He might taste death for everyone (Hebrews 2:9).

Philippians 2:8 states, "And being found in appearance as a man, He [*Jesus*] humbled Himself by becoming obedient to the point of death, even death on a cross."

Not only *could* Jesus die for men, but He was willing to do so. It's one thing to have a friend who *could* give His life for you, but it's quite another thing to find one who *would!*

Jesus was born to die!

We all have death ahead of us as a consequence of our fallen natures. But Jesus knew when He came into the world that His main mission in life was to die for men (Hebrews 10:5-10). What a thing to have hanging over your head all your life! Yet the Bible tells us, it was because of the joy that was set before Him that He endured the shame and pain of the cross (Hebrews 12:2). That joy was the anticipation of removing all the barriers between God and man and bringing about a reconciliation.

3. *God became a man to be a mediator.* A mediator is one who effects a reconciliation between estranged parties. Paul wrote to Timothy, "For there is one God, and one mediator also between God and men, the man Christ Jesus" (1 Timothy 2:5).

Back in the Book of Job the "daysman" or "mediator" showed us that in order to be a go-between, it was necessary to be equal to both persons involved in the mediation (Job 9). The One who could bring man and God back together had to be equal to both.

This qualification narrows it down quickly to only

One in the history of the universe—Jesus Christ, the God-man.

This mediator had to be the sinless Son of God in order to have the quality of righteousness acceptable to a holy God in the mediation. Jesus had that kind of personal perfection, and as a confirmation of that fact, when He was being baptized in the River Jordan, a voice out of heaven spoke saying, "This is My beloved Son, in whom I am well pleased" (Matthew 3:17).

The mediator also had to be able to sympathize with the predicament of man, and thus he had to also be a true man, but a man who never sinned.

Jesus was this man.

4. *God had to become a man to be a priest.* A priest is a man who represents humanity's cause before God. He has to experience all the temptations and trials of men in order to be a sympathetic and knowledgeable intercessor for men.

Six chapters in the Book of Hebrews are devoted to a discussion of the priesthood of Jesus (Hebrews 4,5,7, 8,9,10). But six verses sum up the work of Jesus as mankind's high priest.

"And the former priests [*those who lived in Israel's past history*], on the one hand, existed in greater numbers, because they were prevented by death from continuing [in office], but He [*Jesus*], on the other hand, because He abides forever, holds His priesthood permanently.

"Hence also He is able to save forever those who draw near to God through Him, since He always lives to make intercession for them.

"For it was fitting that we should have such a high priest [*as Jesus*], holy, innocent, undefiled, separated from sinners and exalted above the heavens; who does not need daily, like those high priests [of old], to offer up sacrifices, first for His own sins, and then for the sins of the people, because this He did once for all when He offered up Himself.

"For the Law appoints men as high priests who are weak, but the word of the oath, which came after the

Law, appoints a Son, made perfect forever" (Hebrews 7:23-28).

Jesus is a high priest who's been in our shoes. He knows what it's like to live under the pressures and temptations of this world. "For we do not have a high priest who cannot sympathize with our weaknesses, but one who has been tempted in all things as we are, yet without sin. Let us therefore draw near with confidence to the throne of grace, that we may receive mercy and may find grace to help in time of need" (Hebrews 4:15,16).

5. *He had to become man to be the revealer of God.*
Man, in his spiritual death, had lost any accurate concept of God. God had to become visible to us in terms that our soulish life could grasp, and Jesus is God made real in human form.

Jesus said of Himself, "He who has seen Me has seen the Father. I and the Father are one" (John 14:9; 10:30). In a very real sense, Jesus is a living photograph of the Father. All that God wanted revealed of Himself, He revealed in the Person of His Son, Jesus.

But Jesus is not only the revealer of the Father to man, He's also the revealer of the Father's plan to redeem mankind (Hebrews 1:1-3).

6. *He had to be a man to occupy King David's throne.*
Long ago God promised David He would have a greater son who would reign on his throne over Israel forever (see 1 Chronicles 17:11-15 and Isaiah 9:6,7). So Jesus had to be born as a direct blood descendant of David in order to fulfill that prophecy.

When the angel spoke to Mary about the miraculous conception which was to take place in her womb, he said, concerning the child, "He will be great, and will be called the Son of the Most High; and the Lord God will give Him the throne of his father David; and He will reign over the house of Jacob forever; and His kingdom will have no end" (Luke 1:32,33).

Both Mary and her husband Joseph were direct descendants of King David. Through Mary, Jesus received

the blood right to the throne of David, and through
Mary's husband, Joseph, who acted as Jesus' earthly
father, He received the legal right.

7. *God had to become a man in order to be a "kinsman
redeemer."* This is a concept taught in the Old Testament, especially in the Book of Ruth. In the Law of
Moses, whenever a Jewish person was put into slavery,
the only one who could pay the ransom price to release
him was someone "near of kin" (Leviticus 25:25).
This was to establish the principle that whoever would
be the one to free mankind from its slavery to Satan
would have to be a "near of kin" to the ones being
freed, in this case the human race. In taking on humanity, Jesus became a "kinsman" of men and qualified to be the "kinsman redeemer." This is one of
the reasons that Jesus loved to call Himself the Son of
Man.

Jesus, the God-Man

In the last two chapters we've examined many lines of
evidence that clearly shows why it was necessary for
God to come into this world, clothed with a human
body. We've also seen that the complete humanity
which was prepared for Him to live in while here on
earth for thirty-three years was none other than Jesus
of Nazareth.

Jesus firmly believed he was God, Incarnate (*in the
flesh*). He said that He had come from God (John 6:38,
15; 16:27,28; 17:5) and that He actually was God
(John 10:30; John 20:26-29; Mark 14:61,62). He accepted worship (Matthew 8:2,3; 9:18; 14:33) and told
people that He forgave them of their sins, which only
God had the power to do (Mark 2:5-12; Matthew
9:1-8).

He predicted He would rise from the dead (Matthew
27:62-66; Mark 8:31,32; 9:31), which He did. He
said He was going back to the Father's house to prepare
dwelling places for His children and He would return
personally to the earth and take them with Him into
heaven (John 14:1-3; Acts 1:10,11).

Was He Telling the Truth?

Now, what do you do with a man who said all those things about Himself? You can't dismiss it simply because you don't want to make a judgment as to His truthfulness or sanity. You must come to some conclusion in your own mind about Jesus.

As C.S. Lewis, the brilliant British scholar said of Jesus, in his wonderful book, *Mere Christianity,* "I'm trying here to prevent anyone saying the really foolish thing that people often say about Jesus: *'I'm ready to accept Jesus as a great moral teacher, but I don't accept His claim to be God.'* That is the one thing we must not say. A man who was *merely* a man and said the sort of things Jesus said would not be a great moral teacher. He would either be a lunatic—on the level with the man who says he is a poached egg—or else he would be the Devil of Hell. You must make your choice. Either this man was, and is, the Son of God, or else a madman or something worse. You can shut Him up for a fool, you can spit at Him and kill Him as a demon, or you can fall at His feet and call Him Lord and God. But let us not come up with any patronising nonsense about His being just a great human teacher. He has not left that open to us. He did not intend to." [1]

---

[1] C. S. Lewis, *Mere Christianity* (New York: The Macmillan Company, 1943).

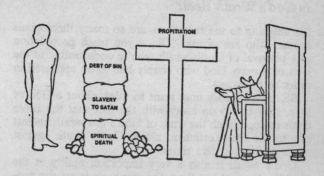

Chapter Nine
Propitiation

In the last two chapters we've looked at why God had to become a man and why it could have been no other man but Jesus.

Now I want to show why Jesus had to go to the cross; why there was no other way for God to reconcile men to Himself.

In the illustration above, I've shown that the first work of Christ on the cross is called "propitiation." Don't be scared by this word. It's a beautiful word which means to "turn away wrath by the *satisfaction* of violated justice." Webster's dictionary defines the word similarly as "to appease and render favorable; to conciliate and reconcile."

You'll notice in the diagram that Christ's act of propitiation has removed the barrier of God's offended character. It's because when Jesus hung on the cross, He bore the compounded fury of God's just wrath against the sins of mankind. Now God has no more wrath to pour out on men. His justice is satisfied that all sin has been paid for.

Propitiation removed God's wrath.

Is God's Wrath Real?

It's amazing to me that there are so many theologians around who are saying, "Oh, if you teach propitiation as a removal of God's wrath, you're contributing to the idea of a petty God who simply has to be appeased in order to be happy."

So, because they only want to think about a God of love, they try to do away with the fact that the Bible deals in depth with the truth of God's just wrath against sin. In the Old Testament alone, God's wrath against sin is mentioned 585 times.[1]

God's wrath is also a very important reality in the New Testament, but there the emphasis is on the propitiation of Christ which has removed God's wrath from mankind. (See John 3:36; Romans 9:22; Ephesians 5:6; Colossians 3:6.)

Because we're human we don't always look at everything in terms of black and white. We let our sympathy blur our judgment at times.

But God, as the sovereign and righteous judge of the universe, must direct His wrath against sin, wherever it's found and in whomever it's found. He can't let His love for man cause Him to compromise His just condemnation of man's sin.

For instance, I know a judge who is a very warm and loving person with real empathy for human needs. He has certainly overlooked and dismissed wrongs done to him in the sphere of his family and friends. But when he is officially in the role of a judge, even though a member of his family has broken the law, he can't sweep the facts under the table and not execute the penalty. If he did, he'd no longer be qualified to judge. A judge who shows partiality and inequity in the administration of the law is unacceptable in any society.

How much more so in the case of God. He's not only

---

[1] For a good Bible study tool both in this area and in general, let me recommend *Young's Analytical Concordance*. If you look up the word "wrath" in this volume, for example, it will show you every place it is used in the Bible and how it is used. It will categorize the English translation with the word in the original language it was written in.

our creator, but also the judge of the universe. As such, He doesn't have the liberty of breaking the very laws which inherently emanate from His character. If He did, the universe would be in chaos. There would be no absolute standards at all that anyone could count on.

No! God's wrath is real, but so is His solution—Christ's propitiatory death on the cross.

Propitiation Propounded

Since this concept of propitiation is so new to many, let's look at it more in depth. The central verses in the New Testament that teach the doctrine of propitiation are Romans 3:25, 26.

There are two important points I want to emphasize about propitiation. First, when the Bible says Christ died to satisfy the offended righteousness and justice of God, and to turn away wrath from those who believe in Him, this even included believers in the Old Testament who lived *before* the cross! That's what it means when it says in that passage, "God passed over the sins previously committed." God put the sins of those Old Testament saints on a charge account which was guaranteed to be paid by the promise of a coming Savior. (See Isaiah 53; Jeremiah 31:31-34.)

But the second emphasis of this passage in Romans 3 is that Jesus was displayed "publicly" as a propitiation. God did this so that the whole world would know that His offended character had been conciliated by Jesus' death and now God had a perfect right to declare righteous all who would believe in His Son's substitutionary death on their behalf.

The Tent in the Wilderness

Perhaps the clearest example in the Bible as to what propitiation means is found in its Old Testament counterpart. The Greek word for "propitiation" is *hilasterion*. This is the same word for the Old Testament Hebrew word, "mercy seat."

The "mercy seat" was part of the furniture God told
Moses to build and set in a special place of worship in
the wilderness. This special worship building was a
portable tentlike affair which served the Hebrews in
their worship of their God while they traveled in the
Sinai Wilderness for forty years. It was called the
"Tabernacle."

This was the place where God came down to meet
with men through the intercession of their high priest,
and it was the place where men came to meet God and
have their sins forgiven through the system of animal
sacrifices which God had instructed Moses to institute.

Everything about this Tabernacle and its articles of
furniture was intended to portray in a temporal way
what God would one day do permanently. The animal
sacrifices were valid until God would one day provide
the lamb of His choosing.

That "Lamb" was His Son, Jesus. As John the Baptist said of Jesus when He saw Him coming toward
him, "Look! Here comes the Lamb of God who will
take away the sins of the world" (John 1:29).

Levi and Sons' Furniture

There were a number of pieces of important furniture
in the two rooms in the Tabernacle which the priestly
tribe of Levi used in their daily intercessions for the
people.

But the most important article in the entire Tabernacle was located in the inner room called the "Holy
of Holies." This was the room where God's presence
dwelt on earth, and it was the place of "propitiation"
for God. The central object in the room was a rather
small acacia wood box, covered with gold. God had
given Moses exact instructions on how to make this
"Ark of the Covenant." You can learn the details of its
construction in Exodus 25.

Everything about this focal piece of furniture was
symbolic of the Person and work of God's coming
Lamb, Jesus Christ. The wood represented His human-

ity, the gold His deity. The top, or lid, of this ark was solid gold and became known as the "mercy seat," which the New Testament word *hilasterion* describes as the place of propitiation.

God left nothing to chance in His detailed blueprint to Moses as to how this Ark of the Covenant was to be constructed. Each tiny part of it held unbelievable symbolic significance in God's eternal plan to redeem fallen mankind.

Extremely significant were the replicas of two angels called "cherubim" made facing each other with outstretched wings, looking down upon the mercy seat. And under this mercy seat, in the ark itself, were three peculiar items described for us in Hebrews 9:1-6.

Manna For All Seasons

First, God told Moses to place inside the ark a pot of manna. You'll remember that manna was a food God provided for the Israelites during their forty-year stint in the wilderness. At first the people had welcomed this miraculous provision, but soon they began griping about it and asked for some variety in their diet.

"Boy, we wish we had some of those delicious foods we had back in Egypt," they murmured.

Their attitude really angered God. After all, no one had gotten sick in those forty years, so it must have been plenty nutritious.

So God said, "Put the manna in the pot and put it in the ark." This became a symbol of man's rejection of God's material provisions.

A Rod to Remember

The second item for the Ark originated from a rebellion within the camp of Israel against Moses' and Aaron's leadership (Numbers 16, 17). After God had dealt with the rebel instigators, He called the tribal leaders to come before Moses. The symbol of leadership was a rod, or wooden staff. Moses took a rod from each tribe and deposited all twelve in the Tabernacle overnight. The man whose rod sprouted leaves was the one God wanted as the leader.

When the rods were taken from the Tabernacle the next day, Aaron's was budded with leaves. But the Israelites disobeyed Aaron's and Moses' leadership anyway, and his rod was placed inside the ark as a reminder of man's refusal of God's leadership.

Stones That Speak

The third item in the ark was the stones upon which the Ten Commandments were inscribed. After Moses had received the two tablets of the Law written by the finger of God, he came down the mountain, only to find the people in rebellion and idolatry. The gross sins of the crowd angered Moses so much, he flung the tablets onto the ground and they smashed into pieces. Later God rewrote them on stone and had them placed inside the ark as the symbol of man's rejection of God's holiness.

The ark, therefore, contained the physical representations of the total sinfulness of man—

> *the manna,* man's rejection of God's earthly provisions;
> *Aaron's rod,* man's rejection of God's leadership;
> *the tablets of the law,* man's rejection of God's holiness.

The Day of Atonement

The Ark of the Covenant was located in the Holy of Holies, the inner chamber of the Tabernacle. Only one man in all the world was allowed in that chamber, the high priest of Israel, and he, only once a year on the Day of Atonement. On that day he would take the blood of an animal sacrifice and sprinkle it over the top of the mercy seat.

Cherubs in the Bible are always associated with the holiness of God, as His guardians and personal servants

(Ezekiel 1; Genesis 3:24). It appears that one of the cherubim hovering over the mercy seat represented the absolute righteousness of God; the other, His perfect justice.

When the cherub of righteousness looked down on the symbols in the ark, it saw all the evidences of man's rejection of God. The cherub of justice saw that man was no longer like God's righteousness, and pronounced the penalty of death upon man.

How Wrath Becomes Mercy

But on the Day of Atonement, what did the angels see? The symbols of sin?

No. They saw the *blood* of a divinely ordained innocent sacrifice covering the symbols of sin. Justice could now say, "I'm satisfied, because the death penalty has been paid." Righteousness said, "I'm no longer offended because the evidence of man's sin has been covered from my eyes and I see only the blood of an innocent substitute who paid the required penalty of death."

One more thing is very important here symbolically. The golden lid (mercy seat) was comparable to being God's throne on earth, because He said He dwelt between the cherubim.

"And there I will meet with you, and from above the mercy seat, from between the two cherubim which are upon the ark of the testimony . . ." (Exodus 25:22).

Until the blood of the animal was sprinkled on the mercy seat, this throne of God depicted a place of judgment. But, covered by the blood once a year, it became a throne of mercy, or mercy seat. God could now sit upon this throne and show the facet of His character called "mercy" because His righteousness and justice were completely satisfied by the blood sacrifice which He had ordained!

"I will appear in the cloud over the mercy seat," God said in Leviticus 16:2. Here was the place where estranged man could now meet God through the mediation of the sacrifice.

The symbolism represented in the sacrificial system and the worship in the Tabernacle is really beautiful. Through this picture the Old Testament believers learned more of the nature of God and His Messiah, and how God would one day perfect His work of salvation.

A Shadow of Things to Come

I've gone into some detail about the Tabernacle, and particularly the Ark of the Covenant, because it's written about them that they are "a copy and shadow of the *heavenly* things." In fact, that's why Moses was warned by God when he was about to build the Tabernacle that he should make everything about it *exactly* according to the pattern God showed him while He was up on Mount Sinai. It was to be a copy and picture of things which actually exist in heaven (Hebrews 8:5).

This command of God takes on great importance when we start analyzing the various functions of the Tabernacle and attempting to see the deeper truths that they were "foreshadowing." We have to keep in mind that whatever was enacted in symbol and type in the *earthly* tabernacle where God dwelt, was either being enacted, or would be in the future, in the *heavenly* tabernacle where God dwells now.

Jesus is the Real Thing

One reason why I usually get bogged down and spend months teaching the lessons of the Tabernacle when I teach Old Testament classes is that every function and symbol of the tabernacle worship found its deeper fulfillment in the life, death, and resurrection of Jesus Christ. Only God could have so perfectly planned such a detailed and minute correlation between the "shadow" and its ultimate reality.

If you want a fascinating and rewarding study of all the ways in which Jesus fulfilled the types pictured in the Tabernacle, I suggest you read Dr. J. Vernon McGee's book, *Tabernacle, God's Portrait of Christ*.[2]

I also suggest a thorough reading of the Book of Hebrews, since it's in this book that much of this typology is unraveled for us.

The New Testament writer who wrote the Book of Hebrews had as his main audience hundreds of Hebrews who had accepted Jesus as the promised Messiah. He himself must have been Jewish since he had such a perfect understanding of the correlation of the Old Testament symbols of worship and Christ's fulfillment of them.

The Only Perfect High Priest

Because our particular interest in this chapter deals with Christ's propitiatory work for man, I want to center on His role as high priest.

In the tabernacle worship, it was the role of the high priest to enter the Holy of Holies once a year and place the blood of an innocent sacrifice onto the mercy seat and thereby obtain God's mercy for the people for another year.

Listen to what the writer of Hebrews says of Jesus,

> But when Christ appeared as a high priest of the good things to come, He entered through the greater and more perfect tabernacle, not made with hands, that is to say, not of this creation; and not through the blood of goats and calves, but through His own blood, He entered the holy place once for all, having obtained eternal redemption (Hebrews 9:11, 12).

The importance of this statement is overwhelming! Jesus, as our high priest, actually entered the Holy of Holies in heaven with the blood of an innocent sacrifice, HIS OWN BLOOD. There He sprinkled it on the mercy seat of the heavenly tabernacle and obtained, not just a temporary, year-long forgiveness for men, but an *eternal* redemption. And it says He did it "once for

[2] J. Vernon McGee, *Tabernacle, God's Portrait of Christ* (Thru the Bible Books).

all," which means it never has to be done again and
again as the former priests had to do.

Think of it!

This one act of Jesus, the High Priest and Lamb, has
forever satisfied God's justice and righteousness. His
infinitely efficacious blood has been put on record at
the throne of God so that it will *forever* remind the
Father that His wrath has already been fully poured
out upon man's sin.

The blood of Jesus is our guarantee that God will
never again be angry with anyone who believes in Jesus as his personal Savior. Jesus' blood has turned
God's throne from one of judgment to one of mercy.

The substitutionary death of Christ has removed the
barrier of God's offended character for all men—the
whole world. God's wrath has been conciliated, and He
is now free to deal with every man individually on the
basis of grace. If a person spends eternity separated
from God, it won't be because of God's wrath. It will
be because he hasn't availed Himself of God's mercy
made available through Jesus' death on the cross.

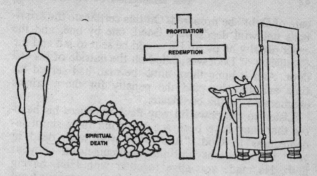

PROPITIATION
REDEMPTION
SPIRITUAL DEATH

Chapter Ten

Redemption

In the last chapter we saw the first barrier between God and man, GOD'S HOLY CHARACTER, being torn down by the propitiation of Christ. That was the work of Christ in presenting His blood at the mercy seat in heaven and obtaining *permanent* forgiveness for men by satisfying the outraged holiness of God.

Redemption is the work of Jesus Christ on our behalf to (1) cancel out the DEBT OF SIN, and (2) release us from SLAVERY TO SATAN and the sin nature. You'll notice in the diagram that these barriers have been torn down by the redemptive work of Christ on the cross.

The Certificate of Debt

In chapter four, when we were discussing how man had incurred his DEBT OF SIN, we saw that the Apostle Paul, in describing this indebtedness, had used a scene right out of the Roman law courts.

Every time a Roman citizen was convicted of a crime, the jurisprudence of the day demanded that a "Certificate of Debt" be prepared. On this certificate the criminal's unlawful deeds were listed, one by one, and the exact penalty he owed. He would be sent to jail and the Certificate of Debt was nailed on the outside of his cell door. And it hung there until the man had served his time and thereby paid the penalty for those crimes enumerated on the certificate.

Listen to the powerful way Paul convinces his hearers that they have been set free from their sinful indebtedness to God. "And when you were dead in your transgressions and the uncircumcision of your flesh, He made you alive together with Him, having forgiven us all our transgressions, having cancelled out the certificate of debt consisting of decrees against us and which was hostile to us; and He has taken it out of the way, having nailed it to the cross" (Colossians 2:13, 14).

Our Certificate of Debt consists of decrees—God's laws which we've broken—and they stand against us. They're "hostile" to us because *we can't keep them*, without breaking some of them. There's nothing wrong with God's laws; they're perfect. The problem lies with our inability to keep them.

Paul gives us a fantastic picture here of Jesus taking your Certificate of Debt and mine and nailing it to the cross. In doing this, it was tantamount to saying He was guilty of every sin listed on every certificate of every man who would ever be born. Not only was He volunteering to take our certificates, but also their penalty which was death.

The Day the Planet Was Liberated

Let's take a brief glance at that day in history that forever altered God and man's relationship—the day Jesus died.

Here's how it happened. Jesus was nailed to the cross at about 9:00 in the morning. He prayed for those who had nailed Him there. Then He made provision for His mother, turning her over to the keeping of His disciple, John. Just before noon He began His dialog with the two criminals on each side of Him, and one of them turned in repentance to the Lord. He was promised a place in paradise, beginning at the moment of his death.

At noonday God drew a veil of darkness over the whole earth. It was pitch black. I believe God did this so that no one would be able to witness visually the horror of what was happening to Jesus as He hung there—because in that moment, the entire wrath of God was engulfing Him as He allowed the sins of all mankind to be put on Him.

Until then Jesus hadn't uttered even a whimper.

But then, all of a sudden, the silence was broken and Jesus cried out in His humanity, *"Eloi, Eloi, lama sabachthani,"* which means, "My God, My God, why have You forsaken Me?"

In that instant God had taken the Certificates of Debt of every human being from the beginning of mankind until the close of history, and nailed them to the cross, making Jesus responsible and guilty for each one!

And God had to turn His back on His own Son in His greatest hour of need, because Christ had voluntarily allowed Himself to be made a sinner on our behalf and God could have no fellowship with sinners of *any* kind until redemption was completed.

When I get to heaven I want to ask Jesus, "Lord, what really happened in that awful hour of blackness?"

Even after He explains it to me, I know I won't be able to comprehend what it must have been like for the poured-out fury of a holy God to fall like an atomic blast on Jesus.

His scream was out of deep agony of soul because, for the first and last time for all eternity, the Second Person of the Godhead, Jesus, was separated from the other two members of the Godhead, the Father and the Spirit.

No one will ever be as alone as Jesus was there on the cross. He was separated from every person He'd ever loved and trusted. Forsaken by His closest friends, forsaken by God the Father and God the Holy Spirit, forsaken by all, He hung there in an aloneness that nobody will ever be able to fathom.

Do you know why He did it?

So that you and I would never have to be alone again. So He could tell those who believed in Him, "I will never desert you, nor will I ever forsake you" (Hebrews 13:5).

The Cry That Shook the World

But that's not the end of the story.

Just before Jesus gave up His earthly life and commended His Spirit to the Father, He shouted a word which is the Magna Carta of all true believers.

That victorious cry was *"Tetelestai!"*

Let that word burn like a firebrand into your mind, because that's the *exact same word* that a Roman judge would write across a released criminal's Certificate of Debt to show that all his penalty had been paid and he was free at last. The word used in this way means "paid in full" and is translated in many Bibles as "It is finished."

In the mind of God, "Paid in Full" has been written across the Certificate of Debt of every man who will ever live because his debt to God has been fully paid by Jesus.

But if a man would be so foolish as to insist on staying imprisoned by his sins, even though his debt has been paid, then the Certificate of Debt assuring his freedom is of no benefit to him. And when he comes to the end of his life, he will have to pay the penalty of death and separation from God himself, even though it's totally unnecessary.

The Other Side of Redemption

Having our DEBT OF SIN canceled is the first benefit of Christ's redemptive work on the cross. But equal to that is the fact that it also released us from SLAVERY TO SATAN and the power of the indwelling sin nature.

The word "redemption" was a very familiar word in the first century since nearly half the world was involved in slavery in one way or another. The sweetest word a slave could hope to hear was the word "redemption."

Since one of the major barriers between God and man is man's SLAVERY TO SATAN, the New Testament writers have freely used the concept of redemption to describe the work of Christ on the cross which has reclaimed man from Satan's clutches.

In the Greek language there are several different words for "redemption" which emphasize different aspects of it. These have all been translated into our one English word "redemption." In order to appreciate fully the scope of freedom from SLAVERY TO SATAN which Christ has purchased for us, let's look at four different emphases of the word "redemption."

Emphasis on Freedom

The first word is a verb, *lutroo*. Its root meaning is "to set free," and its inherent emphasis is the *state of being free*. Since the word means to be set free from slavery by the payment of a ransom, it's translated "redemption."

The word *lutroo* is used in 1 Peter 1:18, 19 as follows: "Knowing that you were not *redeemed* with perishable things like silver or gold from your futile way of life inherited from your forefathers, but with precious blood, as of a lamb unblemished and spotless, the blood of Christ."

Emphasis on Being God's Possession

Another verb is *peripoieo,* which means "redeemed" but is translated "purchased" in Acts 20:28: ". . . shepherd the church of God which He [Jesus] *purchased* [literally: "gained possession of"] with His own blood." Here the emphasis is not on freedom as such, but *on the means to freedom:* the act of buying or gaining possession of something so that it becomes

yours to own. Thus, through redemption we've become
God's personal property.

Emphasis on the Place of Slavery

A third word is *agorazo*, coming from the root noun,
agora, meaning the actual slave market itself. This derived word came to mean "being set free from the
slave market by paying a ransom." It emphasizes the
awfulness of the place from which we're purchased
and is used in Revelation 5:9: "Worthy are You [Je-
sus] . . . for You are slain, and *purchased* for God
with Your blood men from every tribe and tongue and
people and nation."

Emphasis on Permanence of Freedom

Then there's a final verb, which is the intensive form
of *agorazo;* it's *ex*agorazo. The prefix *ex* is added
which means "out of" ("ex" as in "exit") and emphasizes being purchased *out of* the slave market,
never to be sold as a slave again.

The implication here is obvious, as the word is used
in Galations 3:13: "Christ *redeemed* us from the curse
of the Law, having become a curse for us." The Law is a
"curse" to us because we can't keep it, and that has
brought us under SLAVERY TO SATAN and to sin.
But Jesus redeemed us from this curse, having taken the
curse of sin and death for us. Yet in His resurrection,
He once and for all defeated Satan and threw off his
temporary dominion over His humanity.

This Little "Slave" Went to Market

The Word of God graphically pictures mankind as being, not only sinful, but also, as a result, in SLAVERY
TO SATAN in a slave market of sin. The Scriptures
are very clear that there's only one way out of the
dilemma. A redeemer, who is not himself in the slave
market, must redeem all mankind out of it.

That redeemer is Jesus. Here's the picture.

THE SITUATION	THE INTERPRETATION	BIBLE REFERENCE
The Slave Market	The World System	1 John 5:19
The Slave Master	Satan	John 12:31
The Slaves	Humanity	Eph. 2:2, 3
The Problem	Sin	Col. 2:14
The Highest Bidder	Jesus (Redeemer)	Heb. 2:14, 15
The Ransom Price	Blood of Christ	1 Pet. 1:18, 19

Jesus said, "Every one who commits sin is the slave of sin" (John 8:34). Since everyone commits sin (if you ever run into somebody who says he doesn't, check around with his friends!), we're all slaves. It's a condition we're born into with Satan as the father and head of the fallen race of mankind (John 8:44). He energizes the unbelievers (Ephesians 2:1-4), and He empowers the whole world system as well (1 John 5:19).

Have you ever wondered why the world's in the mess it's in?

Consider the source!

The evil in the world is not just some impersonal force. We're dealing with the reality of a personal being so influential that the whole world has fallen prey to his devices. "For our struggle is not against flesh and blood, but against the rulers, against the powers, against the world-forces of this darkness, against spiritual forces of wickedness in the heavenly [atmospheric] places" (Ephesians 6:12).[1]

Jesus, the Liberator!

Into this insane "slave market of sin" God sent a redeemer to "open [men's] eyes so that they may turn from darkness to light and from the dominion of Satan to God" (Acts 26:18). But Jesus didn't just "happen along"; it was by careful design in the plan of God. God couldn't select just anyone to be the liberator of

[1] See author's book, *Satan Is Alive and Well on Planet Earth*, for more details (Zondervan Publishing House, 1972).

mankind; he had to meet the qualifications of a redeemer.

And Jesus perfectly did!

In the Roman system of slavery, every citizen of
the empire knew that a slave couldn't free himself, nor
could he be freed by another slave. It took a free man
with an authentic and proper ransom to do it.

In the same way, no human being can free another
because we're all in the slave market together. The
services of a qualified outsider—One chosen by God—
are required, as we discussed in chapters seven and
eight.

Let's briefly review the qualifications of Jesus as the
redeemer of mankind.

Sinless Redeemer

First of all, the one who would redeem men from Satan's slavery had to be without sin himself. After warn-
ing His listeners of their slavery to sin, Jesus says, "The
slave does not remain in the house forever; the son
does remain forever" (John 8:35).

In other words, the son is a permanent part of the
household, the slave is not. And since the son is above
the slave, he has authority over the slave and could
even set him free if he chose to.

And then Jesus pulls a fantastic play on words. He
says, in the very next verse, "If therefore the Son shall
make *you* free, you shall be free indeed." In saying
this to them, He is equating them with being slaves
and is, in essence, telling them that He is the Son and
He alone has the power to set them, the sin-slaves,
free.

As we've seen already, Christ is the only man to be
born on this earth since Adam who was not Himself a
slave to sin. That's because of His unique conception.
God was the father of His humanity, and Jesus' mother
was a virgin. Since the culpability for sin is passed
from human father to child, Jesus by-passed inherited
sin because His "family tree" on His Father's side was

not human, but divine. Jesus also lived a life that was completely sinless.

Thus Jesus met the first qualification for being a redeemer. He Himself was a free man and the only one capable of paying the ransom price.

Kinsman Redeemer

Secondly, the redeemer had to be "next of kin" to the human race. Hebrews 2:14,15 explains why this was so: "Since then the children [mankind] share in flesh and blood, He Himself likewise also partook of the same [flesh and blood], that through death He might render powerless him who had the power of death, that is, the devil; and might deliver those who through fear of death were subject to slavery all their lives."

You see, the price of redemption for man has always been the shed blood of an innocent substitute. Moses taught in the Law, "Without the shedding of blood, there is no remission of sin" (Hebrews 9:22). However, the blood of animals could never take the sin away; it only atoned for, or covered it, temporarily until God provided a complete remission of sins through His ultimate sacrifice of Jesus (Hebrews 10:11-14).

But, since the redemption price had to be the shed *blood* of an *innocent* sacrifice, the redeemer had to be someone with blood in his veins who could actually experience death. In other words, a man, but one who was completely innocent of any sins.

That's why we read about Christ's death in 1 Peter 1:19, that it accomplished redemption "with precious blood, as of a lamb *unblemished* and *spotless*, the blood of Christ."

Mediating Redeemer

Third, the redeemer had to be a mediator, one who was equal to both parties in the mediation—those in the slave market, and the One seeking to release the slaves. In other words, the redeemer needed to be both

God and man. "For there is one God, and one mediator also between God and men, the man Christ Jesus,
who gave Himself as a *ransom* for all" (1 Timothy
2:5,6).

Willing Redeemer

Finally, in order for a person to become a redeemer,
he must do so voluntarily. Certainly a slave was in no
position to order a free man to liberate him. The free
man would have to be motivated somehow to come
and pay the ransom.

When speaking of the life He was to give as a sacrifice for sin, Jesus told the Pharisees in John 10:17,
18, "I lay down My life that I may take it again. No
one takes it away from Me, but I lay it down on My
own initiative."

The reason why?

His love for you and me!

That love is what sent Him to the cross, canceling
our DEBT OF SIN and purchasing us out of SLAV-
ERY TO SATAN. These are no longer barriers between God and man:

Unless we let them be!

From Jesus, With Love!

The redemption that Jesus made available to men at
the cross is a love gift with no strings attached. We're
not used to receiving things without someone wanting
something in return, so it's hard to really grasp the
nature of this fantastic offer of a free salvation. In the
back of many peoples' minds is the thought that there
must be a hidden gimmick somewhere. No one gives
something for nothing!

But let me assure you, there's no fine print in the
contract of salvation. It doesn't even say that we have
to give Him ourselves. All we're asked to do is to *take*
the pardon He's graciously offered us and then begin
to enjoy our freedom.

Jesus said, "Come to Me all you who labor and are heavily burdened, and *I will give you rest*" (Matthew 11:28, Modern Language Bible). All we have to do is come to Him, give Him our burdens, and take the gift of rest from Him.

John wrote, "As many as received Him [Jesus], *to them God gave the power* to become the children of God, even to those who believe in His name" (John 1:12). Here again we're asked only to believe in what Jesus did for us in providing our liberation at the cross, and then God gives us the power to become His children.

The Tragedy of the "Might-Have-Been"

As much as I hate to, I must add this final note to this chapter on redemption. Just because Christ has redeemed all mankind from Satan's slave market of sin, unfortunately not everyone has chosen to avail himself of the ransom and go free.

The story is told of a young man who was convicted of murder in an eastern state many years ago. His parents, being influential and wealthy, finally obtained a stay of execution from the governor, and eventually the convict was granted a pardon.

This man, still sitting on death row, was given the news that he had been given his freedom. But when he was handed the pardon, he rejected it. He said, "I'm guilty and I want to die."

Try as they could, his family and lawyers couldn't persuade him to change his mind. In an effort to keep him from being executed, the family took the case all the way to the highest court in the state. And the court ruled that a pardon is not a pardon until it is accepted by the one for whom it was intended.

So the man went to his death, not because he had no alternative, but because he refused to accept the pardon.

So it is with men. Those who spend eternity separated from God in bitter anguish of soul and body will do so, not because there isn't an alternative, but because they won't accept the pardon that has already been made available.

But once a man accepts the pardon, he's forever free. And not just after he dies, either. He's free in this life, in the here-and-now as well as the sweet-by-and-by.

If you've never done so before, why not right this moment thank Jesus Christ for dying for *you,* personally, and accept His gracious pardon and forgiveness. You'll be eternally glad you did!

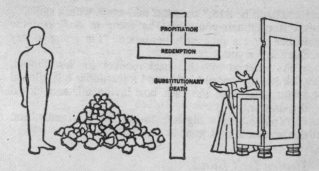

Chapter Eleven

Substitutionary Death

Billy Graham, in an address at Yale University, told the story of how he was driving through a small town in the South one evening and was picked up by radar in a speed trap. He was clocked at several miles over the limit.

A squad car pulled him over and instructed him to follow the car to the local justice of the peace. The justice happened to be a barber, and the office was right there in the barber shop.

Graham tells how he walked into the place and the justice was busy shaving a man. He took his time and finished the job. Then he turned to Graham and quickly reviewed his case. "How do you plead?" the justice asked.

"Guilty, your honor," Graham said.

"That'll be $15," replied the justice.

Graham reached for his wallet to pay the fine.

The justice shot him a second glance and said, "Say, aren't you Billy Graham, the evangelist?"

"I regret to say, sir, that I am," Graham responded, hopefully tucking the wallet back into his pocket.

"That'll be $15," the man said again with a smile.

"But I'll tell you what I'm going to do," said the justice after a moment's hesitation. "I'm going to pay the fine for you."

He reached into his back pocket for his billfold, took it out, removed a five and a ten-dollar bill, slipped them underneath the cash box in the till, and closed the drawer.

"You've been a big help to me and my family, and this is something I want to do," he said.

Justice Isn't Blind

The law had been broken, the penalty assessed, and the fine *had* to be paid.

But in this case, as in the case of God versus mankind, a substitute came forward and volunteered to pay the fine. It didn't cost Billy Graham's "savior" much to pay Billy's fine, but the cost to God to provide a savior to pay our "fine" of death, was the death of His Son, Jesus, in our place.

Substitutionary death is the subject of this chapter. This is the work of Christ on the cross that removed forever the barrier of SPIRITUAL DEATH which hangs over the head of every man who's ever been born. It not only has removed our death penalty, but it's made it possible for God to *restore* His life to every man who will accept it.

Just to review it briefly:

Propitiation is toward *God*, satisfying His absolute righteousness and holiness. Christ's death did that for us.

Redemption is toward *sin*, providing payment of the sin-debt through Jesus' blood. As a result, man has also been set free from the slave market of sin and brought out from under Satan's authority. Christ's death did that for us.

Substitutionary death is toward *death*, through Christ's dying in our place. This is the work of Christ we want to look at in depth now.

Sin's Inescapable Penalty

The penalty for sin has always been death. One of the first principles Adam and Eve ever learned from God was that on the day they ate of the forbidden fruit, they would die (Genesis 2:17). They didn't fully understand that "death" meant a spiritual separation from God.

Then on that sad day when Adam and Eve stood over the lifeless body of their dead son, Abel, they were all too aware of what it meant to die physically.

The final aspect of death is still future and is called "the second death" or eternal death. This will be the final eternal state of all who die on this earth without ever having their spiritual lives restored. This is *not* a state of eternal unconsciousness, but rather one of very real torment and remorse for ever and ever (Revelation 20:14,15; Matthew 8:12; Luke 16:19-31).

The Concept of Sacrifice

In each layer of civilization which the archaeologists' spades have uncovered, there have been evidences of sacrifices made to gods. Since many of these scholars have *not* been prone to accept the Biblical concept of divine creation and the subsequent fall of man, they've used the presence of these numerous artifacts of sacrifice to ridicule and discredit the biblical claim of the efficacy of animal sacrifice.

They would claim that the Hebrews were only one race out of many who evolved a system of sacrifice to appease a god they couldn't fathom. And they would point to sacrificial evidence that predated the appearance of the Hebrew race in their effort to disprove any merit in the biblical concept of animal sacrifice for sins.

But how you interpret the relics in the archaeologist's shovel is entirely dependent on the basic premise you have as to the origin of things. If you believe that man is in a process of evolution from a one-celled organism to some glorious superhuman creature of the future, then you would tend to discount the biblical claim of the fall of man and a subsequent *downward* devolution or degeneration.

But if you accept the biblical claim that God created man full grown, in His own image, and that man distorted that image in himself by disobeying God and thereby incurring a penalty of death, then you'll see that the concept of substitutionary sacrifice was a necessary *immediate* intervention of God to reestablish fellowship with man.

It would then be understandable also as to why every stage of human history has its record of animal and human sacrifices. It's because there was an original prototype at the very beginning of human history from which all the other patterns developed, some staying close to the original type and others evolving into bizarre perversions.

The Biblical History of Sacrifice

The account of animal sacrifice found in the Old Testament Book of Genesis occurred long before God gave the command to Moses to institute a system of worship which included animal sacrifices.

The first time an innocent animal had to die because of man's sin was when God killed at least one animal, and possibly several, in the Garden of Eden, to provide a covering for Adam and Eve's nakedness. They had attempted to cover themselves with leaves, but in God's rejecting their feeble effort to hide their guilt from Him, He established a principle that an innocent substitute must die to provide a temporary covering of man's sinfulness.

Although this is not spelled out in detail by Moses in his writing of the Book of Genesis, it's obvious from succeeding records of animal sacrifice that God must have explained this substitutionary-death concept to Adam, and then Adam to his children.

Genesis records the fact that Abel, Noah, Abraham, Isaac, Job, and Jacob all offered sacrifices to God before the time of Moses and the institution of the tabernacle worship (Genesis 4:4; 8:20; 12:7; 26:25; 33:20; Exodus 12:3-11; Job 1:5; 42:7-9).

So the necessity of seeking God's forgiveness of sins through the sacrifice of an innocent substitute was a familiar practice from the very beginning of man's history on this earth. And it was a symbolism instituted by God Himself.

It's also thrilling to me to see how God developed the concept of the substitutionary death of *one lamb for one man* to the ultimate goal of *one lamb for the whole world.*

One Lamb for One Man

God initially authorized the slaying of one animal to atone for the sins of one man. This is pictured for us in the story of Adam's son, Abel's sacrificial offering to God. His brother, Cain, brought an offering of fruit to God, but it was rejected. Obviously, God had previously given instructions through Adam that blood must be shed in order to provide a covering for sins. Abel brought the right sacrifice, and it so angered his brother Cain that he killed him (see Genesis 3:4; Hebrews 11:4).

One Lamb for One Family

In the story of the Passover experience of the Hebrews in Egypt we see that God ordained that one lamb could suffice as a sacrifice for one family (Exodus 12:3-14).

The Passover referred to the night when God had Moses tell Pharaoh that if he didn't let the Hebrews go out of their slavery in Egypt, the first-born of all animals and families in the land (both Hebrew and Egyptian) would die as the death angel passed over Egypt.

In order to spare the Hebrews the death of their first-born, God made the provision that they could kill a lamb and sprinkle its blood over the door and on the two doorposts. Then when the death angel passed over the land of Egypt that night, wherever he saw the blood, he would *pass over* that house and those inside would be spared God's judgment.

God commanded that this Passover day be celebrated yearly as a reminder of God's provision for the salvation of those who sacrificed their lamb for their family.

One Lamb for a Nation

After the Jews left their servitude in Egypt and were on their way to the promised land, God met Moses on Mount Sinai and gave him the ten commandments and many other laws by which the people were to regulate their lives and their worship.

Principally Moses was commanded to construct a portable building which was to be used in their worship and sacrificing to God. This was called the "Tabernacle."

It was made up of an outside court in which there was an altar for the animal sacrifices. There were two rooms on the inside. The first room was called the "Holy Place" and had several articles of furniture that were involved in the worship of God. The innermost room was the most important spot in the Tabernacle. It was called the "Holy of Holies," and it was where the Ark of the Covenant was kept and where the presence of God dwelt above the ark in a blaze of light called "Shekinah Glory."

It was in this Holy of Holies that God ordained that the blood of one sacrificial lamb could atone for the sins of the whole nation of Israel from year to year. It was the job of the high priest to select a perfect animal once a year and take the blood of it into the Holy of Holies and sprinkle it on the mercy seat. In so doing, it conciliated God's wrath against the nation for another year by atoning for the sins of the people. This day came to be called the "Day of Atonement."

One Lamb for the World

Jesus' cousin, John the Baptist, was the first person to call Jesus by the name "Lamb of God." When he saw Jesus coming toward him one day, he said, "Behold, the Lamb of God who takes away the sin of the world" (John 1:29).

Now, where do you suppose John got that mental picture of Jesus as a lamb, taking away the sins of the world?

No doubt in his knowledge of the Old Testament scriptures and his experience with animal sacrifice in the Temple in Jerusalem, he had come to realize that the continual shedding of the blood of substitutionary animals did *not* take away sins or the guilt they produced. He must have sensed that God had made some other provision for forgiveness and cleansing. I'm sure also that God must have supernaturally revealed to him that here was the One who would be that permanent provision for sin.

A few years after this incident with John and Jesus, the writer of the Book of Hebrews explained the whole reason why Jesus was called the "Lamb of God" who takes away the world's sins. I'm going to let him tell you in his own words, because he was obviously Jewish and had experienced some of the frustration of the empty religious treadmill of a sacrificial worship system that didn't really deal with the problem of sin.

You'll notice the number of times he contrasts the old way of doing things with a new one which Jesus instituted. He makes very clear that the old system of approaching God through the blood of animals was never satisfactory to man or God. And then he convincingly sets forth the fact that Jesus was the permanent sacrifice that God had in mind all the time.

The old system of Jewish laws gave only a dim foretaste of the good things Christ would do for us. The sacrifices under the old system were repeated again and again, year after year, but even so they could never save those who lived under their rules. If they could have, one offering would have been enough; the worshipers would have been cleansed once for all, and their feelings of guilt would be gone.

But just the opposite happened: those yearly sacrifices reminded them of their disobedience and guilt instead of relieving their minds. For it is not possible for the blood of bulls and goats really to take away sins.

That is why Christ said, as He came into the world, "O, God, the blood of bulls and goats cannot satisfy you, so you have made ready this body of mine for me to lay as a sacrifice upon your altar. You were not satisfied with the animal sacrifices, slain and burnt before you as offerings for sin. Then I said, 'See, I have come to do your will, to lay down my life, just as the Scriptures said that I would.' "

After Christ said this, about not being satisfied with the various sacrifices and offerings required under the old system, he then added, "Here I am. I have come to give my life."

He cancels the first system in favor of a far better one. Under this new plan we have been forgiven and made clean by Christ's dying for us once and for all. Under the old agreement the priests stood before the altar day after day offering sacrifices that could never take away our sins.

But Christ gave himself to God for our sins as one sacrifice for all time, and then sat down in the place of highest honor at God's right hand, waiting for his enemies to be laid under his feet. For by that one offering he made forever perfect in the sight of God all those whom he is making holy (Hebrews 10:1-14 Living Bible).

Jesus Died Twice

When Jesus was hanging on the cross as our substitute, the writer of Hebrews tells us, it was that "He might taste death for every one" (Hebrews 2:9). Since man's penalty for being a sinner is both spiritual and physical death, Jesus had to taste both kinds of death.

When He shouted out, "My God, My God, why have You forsaken Me?" at that moment, there on the cross, He was actually made sin for us, and in His human spirit He died spiritually.

The Apostle Paul referred to this when he said, "He made Him [Jesus] who knew no sin *to be sin on our behalf,* that we might become the righteousness of God in Him" (2 Corinthians 5:21).

This doesn't mean Jesus was actually sinful in Himself. It means He was treated by the Father as if He were actually sinful. Since Jesus was bearing our sins, God had to judge Him just as He would have had to judge us because of our sins.

In dying spiritually and physically as our substitute, God looked at Jesus' death and credited it to the account of fallen humanity. His spiritual death means God can give spiritual life to all men who will receive it; and His physical death, and defeat of it in the resurrection, means God can ultimately raise our physical bodies and give them immortality.

God's Ultimate Lamb

There's little more that can be said to amplify this vivid picture of Jesus' substitutionary death on our behalf. The only thing to add is that in becoming a Lamb for the world's sins, Jesus *fulfilled the need* for one lamb for a man, one lamb for a family, and one lamb for a nation.

It was no mere coincidence that His crucifixion took place on the day of Passover. He was destined by God to be the world's Passover Lamb whose blood, when applied to the doorposts of our hearts, would cause God to "pass over" us in judgment.

He was also the fulfillment of the lamb on the Day of Atonement upon whom the sins of the people were laid and who was slain in their behalf.

Why?

The only question that might come to mind is, "Why did He do it?"

Jesus gave us the answer to that question when He told His disciples, "Greater love has no one than this, that one lay down his life for his friends" (John 15:13).

Jesus died for us because He loved us!

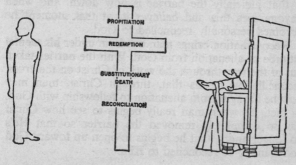

PROPITIATION
REDEMPTION
SUBSTITUTIONARY DEATH
RECONCILIATION

Chapter Twelve

Reconciliation

To me, one of the happiest words in the English language is "reconciliation." I immediately picture two people being restored into a new relationship.

It's one of God's favorite words too, because it means He can now restore man into fellowship with Himself because of the sum total of the threefold work of Christ on the cross:

1. *Propitiation* brings man out from under the wrath of God through satisfying His righteousness and justice.

2. *Redemption* brings man out from slavery to sin and Satan through the payment of a ransom.

3. *Substitutionary Death* brings man out from under the penalty of death through the death of Christ in our place.

The above three have torn down the barrier that man's sin has built up against God. But even with the *barrier* gone, the *relationship* between God and man must be reestablished. This is the work of reconciliation.

You see, God hasn't changed; He's always loved man and still does. The world hasn't changed either;

115

it's still in rebellion against God. But what has changed is that judicially the barrier is now down, and when anyone sees this and *believes* it, at that moment he becomes personally reconciled to God.

Reconciliation brings man out from under his mental attitude of alienation from God. With the barrier taken out of the way through the work of Christ on the cross, reconciliation means that, through Christ, man may now be brought from alienation to fellowship with God. In fact, it's when man really begins to see how Christ has so completely removed the barrier so that He's no longer angry, that he begins to open up toward God and want to be reconciled to Him.

The Greeks Have a Word for it!

You've heard the statement, "The Greeks have a word for it." The Greek language has many words to every one in the English. It was the most explicit language ever devised in the history of the human race. I'm sure it's no mere accident that this was the language God chose for the writing of the New Testament.

There are three words in the Greek language expressing the idea of reconciliation, and all are translated by the one English word "reconciliation."

Word No. 1

The word *daillassomai* means to change two people to friendship who are *both* at odds with each other. It's used that way in Matthew 5:24. ". . . first be reconciled to your brother, and then come and present your offering." Here the parties or "brothers" have turned their backs on each other; both are angry and need to be reconciled.

This word is *never* used with reference to God, because it's we who have turned our backs on God, not He on us!

Word No. 2

The second word for reconciliation is *apokatallasso*. It's closely aligned with the main verb we want to consider, and it means a change completely from enmity to fellowship. When this word is used it means that only one person has been at enmity and that person has been completely restored to fellowship with another.

Word No. 3

The word we'll spend the most time considering is the third word, *katallasso*. This word, meaning to change from enmity to fellowship, is used several places in the New Testament. It's used throughout 2 Corinthians 5:17-21, the key passage on reconciliation.

Katallasso (reconciliation) views it this way: here is God; here is man. Man is at odds with God; he's turned his back on God. God never had to be reconciled; it was man who needed to be. *Katallasso* means only one person in a relationship has turned away and needs to be brought back—just one.

Hosea and the Hooker

The perfect example of the story of reconciliation is the Old Testament Book of Hosea, especially the first few chapters. I call the book the "Romance of Reconciliation." Here's why.

God told Hosea to marry a certain woman He had picked out for him. The woman God chose was a prostitute. Hosea married her and treated her with love and respect. She bore his children.

Then one day she ran off from him and returned to being a prostitute. God told Hosea to go and find her and bring her back.

He finally found his wife on the block at a slave auction. She stood there at the mercy of the bidders, stripped naked—the custom of the day for the auctioning of female slaves—waiting to be sold into slavery. Hosea bought back his own wife, clothed her, brought her back home, and kept right on loving her with no retribution at all.

What a picture! Hosea learned experientially just how God felt about Israel, how Israel's love affairs with pagan gods hurt Him, and now He would stop at nothing to bring these people back.

But this is also a picture of what man has done to God and of what God has done to bring us back. It's a picture of *real* love. You see, Hosea never stopped loving his wife; it was she who turned from him. And the idea is given that Hosea's great love absolutely overwhelmed his wife. She couldn't get over the fact that he still loved her.

As a picture of reconciliation, the Book of Hosea is a Rembrandt!

God never had to be reconciled! He's like Hosea. But it's man who has to be brought back and reconciled, and that's what this word *katallasso* means.

Like Hosea, God knew we would never be brought back to Him unless (a) God took the initiative and (b) God took us "just as we are" in our condition of sin. Hosea didn't try to clean up his wife before he brought her home, nor did she try to clean herself up. She came just as she was and the clean-up took place later.

I'm sure Gomer, Hosea's wife, must have been filled with guilt and shame when she heard Hosea bidding for her at the slave auction. After he got her home, her sense of unworthiness and guilt probably produced an attitude of suspicion and alienation toward Hosea, wondering when he was going to get even with her.

But as the days went by and all that Gomer got from Hosea was love and acceptance, her hostility turned to love and gratitude and she became a love-slave of his.

Reconciliation Neutralizes Hostility

True reconciliation always does away with hostility.

That's what the Apostle Paul was speaking of when he said, "And although you were *formerly* alienated and hostile in mind, engaged in evil deeds, yet He has now reconciled you in His fleshly body through death" (Colossians 1:21, 22).

If we think someone is holding something against us, then we'll feel alienated and hostile toward them, simply out of self-defense. It's even more true when it comes to God. If we feel our sins are still an issue between us and God, then we won't feel like coming to Him because we know how He feels about sin.

But listen to this terrific good news from the pen of the Apostle Paul: "God was in Christ reconciling the world to Himself, *not counting their trespasses against them*, and He has committed to us the word of reconciliation" (2 Corinthians 5:19).

Did you get it? God isn't holding our sins against us anymore. The reconciliation He made available to us through the cross has neutralized His just anger at our sins.

That's why the "cross" must always be the central message of the Gospel, because it's what Christ did there that makes reconciliation with God possible. And without reconciliation there's no way to remove the alienation and hostility that we have in our minds toward God.

When we find out how totally God has done away with the barrier that separated us from Him, and that He isn't mad at us, then we're going to want to "come home" like Hosea's wife did. And when we "come home," we're so grateful for the lack of recrimination and the complete acceptance, that all we want to do is serve our Master.

The Wayward Son Comes Home

Another beautiful illustration of reconciliation is the parable that Jesus told about the prodigal son (Luke 15).

It's important to get the setting of this incident or a

great deal of its meaning is lost. Jesus was teaching, and the biggest part of His audience were tax-gatherers and self-admitted sinners. Interspersed among them were some of the pious super-religious Pharisees and scribes, and they began to make snide remarks about Jesus' friendship with sinners.

Jesus tells three parables to this group, the purpose of which is to teach what God's attitude is toward those who recognize that they are sinners. You see, the Pharisees were sinners, but they didn't think they were. So Jesus was trying to show them that it's better to admit you're a sinner and place yourself under God's grace, than to bravely defend your self-righteousness and miss out on God's blessing.

In this particular parable of the prodigal or way-ward son, there was a father with two sons. The younger one decided he wanted his inheritance so he could leave home and live it up (He represents the publicans and sinners). The older son (representing the self-righteous Pharisees) stayed at home and continued to work for his father (who represents God in this story).

The younger son went into a far-off country and squandered all his inheritance with wild living. A severe famine came in that land, and he found himself in real need. So he hired out to a certain citizen and found himself out in the fields feeding pigs (this citizen was Satan).

Finally the kid said to himself, "This is ridiculous! I'm here starving and my father's slaves have better food than this. I'll go to my father and tell him, 'Father, I know I've sinned against heaven and you by the stupid way I've blown my inheritance, and I'm not even worthy to be a son of yours. But if you'll let me come home, I'll be glad just to be one of your servants.' "

You can tell by what he said that he expected his father to want to have nothing to do with him after the way he'd disappointed him. But he was in for a big surprise!

While he was still a long way from his father's house,

his dad caught sight of him. It's obvious the father must have been hopefully keeping an eye out for him ever since he left. And when he saw him, he ran to the son and threw his arms around him and kissed him.

Then the boy gave him the speech he'd planned about not being worthy, and being willing to come home as a hired man.

But the father never heard a word he said, for he was already giving instructions to the servants to get a big welcome-home party ready. There was no resentment or wrath in the father toward that boy, even though there was plenty of reason for him to be upset.

The father's attitude was expressed in his statement to everyone, "This son of mine was dead and has come to life again. He was lost and has been found."

Reconciliation Isn't "Reasonable"

This parable is such a terrific illustration of reconciliation. Obviously this father dearly loved this boy all his life or he never would have given him his inheritance before it was due, as he had asked. During all those long months and possibly years, the father kept on loving the boy and yearning for him to come home and be reconciled to him.

When the boy recognized how foolish he'd been, he expected there to be stern barriers between him and his father if he wanted to come home. But when he got to the place of willingness to come back to his dad, he found that instead of being barriers there, there was nothing but love and complete acceptance.

Don't Miss the Point

There are certain very important truths which this parable teaches, but there are also some very strong things it *doesn't* teach.

First of all, keep in mind that it is a parable. This was one of Jesus' favorite teaching devices. In a parable, each character generally represented some true person or situation.

In this parable of the prodigal son, the most important thing it doesn't teach is that we're all sons of God, some of whom have simply gone astray. The persons represented by the wayward son were the self-admitted sinners, and these were people who still needed to get right with God.

All men are *creatures* of God and, as such, the objects of His love. Man was once in a relationship of intimacy with God, but has been in a position of straying and rebellion since Adam's fall. And the fact that the father says of his son that he was "dead and is now alive, was lost and is now found" shows that a very radical change had taken place in the relationship of these two.

The change that had taken place is called "reconciliation."

Be Ye Reconciled! ! !

But reconciliation is worth nothing unless the barriers that caused it in the first place are torn down, and then the one who is alienated decides to become reconciled. The prodigal son had to decide to renounce the rebellious life he'd chosen and to go home. That's simply called "repenting," which means to "change your mind and your direction."

Hosea's wife had run from him, but when he came to get her, she had to be willing to go back home with him.

By these four mighty works of Christ on the cross,

     propitiation (1 John 2:2),
     redemption (1 Timothy 2:5, 6),
     substitutionary death (Hebrews 2:9),
     reconciliation (2 Corinthians 5:19),

God has made all men "reconcilable,," but the effect of these truths becomes a reality only when a person believes them. 1 Timothy 4:10 says, "We have fixed our hope on the living God, who is the Savior of all men, *especially of believers.*"

Just how a person becomes personally reconciled to God is a matter of the greatest importance. Our whole eternal destiny depends upon the right decision in this matter. The next chapter will carefully discuss this most important question we must answer: "Have I personally been reconciled to God?"

Chapter Thirteen
A Decision of Destiny

In the last four chapters we saw the wonders of God's love by which He has removed all the barriers between Himself and man.

But the really incredible thing is that God has accomplished a total provision of salvation for even those human beings whom He knew would reject it.

God so loved the "world" that He gave His son (John 3:16). It wasn't just for the part of the world that He knew would receive His salvation that He died. It was for all of those who would ridicule His name, ignore His salvation, despise His Word, and reject His authority.

Whether they want to be or not, the whole world has been made "savable" because of the death of Christ on the cross.

But being "savable" and being "saved" are two different things.

If someone has put $100,000 in a bank account for you, it won't do you any good unless, first of all, you know about it, and secondly, you draw upon it.

The four great doctrines of Christ's death in man's

behalf are for the whole world, but applicable only to those who draw upon it personally.

Propitiation

"He Himself [Jesus] is the propitiation for our sins; and not for ours only, but also *for those of the whole world*" (1 John 2:2).

Redemption

"For there is one God, and one mediator also between God and men, the man Christ Jesus, who gave Himself *a ransom for all*" (1 Timothy 2:5, 6).

Substitutionary Death

"But we do see Him who has been made for a little while lower than the angels, namely, Jesus, because of the suffering of death crowned with glory and honor, that by the grace of God, He might *taste death for every one*" (Hebrews 2:9).

Reconciliation

"God was in Christ *reconciling the world to Himself, not counting their trespasses against them . . .*" (2 Corinthians 5:19).

I once heard a speaker liken God's worldwide offer of salvation to a pet-store owner who puts a free kitten in the window of his shop. It's available to everyone, but it only becomes the possession of the one who goes in and takes it.

God has put His offer of "free forgiveness" in His window and it's *available* to everyone, but only the possession of those who come in and take it.

Don't Get the Cart Before the Horse!

Now, in light of the fact that the barriers have been removed from between God and man, and God freely offers a new relationship with Himself, what must a man do to receive the results of this and have it be a reality in his own life?

At no other point is it more important to distinguish between the *means* of coming into God's salvation and the *effects* of it. It's of utmost importance that we don't get the cart before the horse in the matter of *how* to appropriate all that Christ accomplished for us on the cross.

If we make something which the Bible calls a *result* of salvation part of the *means* by which it's obtained, then we insert human merit into the picture of God's redemptive plan. And human merit nullifies the whole concept of a *free* salvation.

Now let's take a look at some of the things that men have tried to add to "faith" as an additional means of salvation.

Faith, Plus Works?

The Apostle Paul, knowing that all men have an insatiable self-centeredness that makes them want to boast of their spiritual or moral prowess, wrote to the believers in Ephesus, "For by *grace* you have been saved through faith; and *that not of yourselves*, it is the gift of God; *not as a result of works*, that no one should boast" (Ephesians 2:8, 9).

It's a real commentary on the nature of the human heart that at the very outset of Christianity, Paul has to admonish people that salvation is a free gift from God and there's no possible way to do anything to merit it, or else human pride and boasting would come in.

You see, if there were anything God required of man in the way of good deeds or human effort in order to receive God's salvation, then there would be good reason for some people to boast about how they'd helped themselves get into God's family. Because, obviously some people would work much harder than others to obtain God's favor and it follows that it would only be fair that He give them more love and acceptance than the ones who didn't work too hard at it.

Grace: God's Riches At Christ's Expense

But over and over we keep running into a word in the New Testament that tells us the true basis on which God accepts us. That word is "grace."

If we could have only a half-dozen words in our human vocabulary, that word should be one of them. It's one of those words that's so loaded with meaning, you feel as if you need fifty words just to begin to explain it.

But simply put, it means to *freely give something to someone which he can in no possible way deserve or merit or earn.*

The minute there's even a shadow of a hint of someone trying to merit or earn the thing being given, then it's not grace any longer (see Romans 11:6).

Now, what is it that God has given to us that we can't in any way merit?

His love, forgiveness, righteousness, acceptance, mercy, redemption, and eternal life—all of which are wrapped up in one package called "salvation." This is what He's given to us, if we'll take it, and it's given completely on the basis of "grace."

My first brush, on the human level, with the concept of grace was when I got my first health insurance policy. After paying ten hard-earned bucks a month for a couple of years on this policy, I came to a place where I just couldn't scrape together ten dollars one month. I hated to let the policy lapse, because I'd paid so much on it already and I'd never used it once.

But when the payment date arrived, I just didn't send them anything and I sadly figured that would be the last I'd hear of them. Yet, after a couple of weeks I got a letter from them telling me that my policy hadn't been canceled and I was in a thirty-day "grace" period.

I didn't deserve that thirty extra days of coverage, and I hadn't paid for it, but I found out that I was fully covered anyway in case any sickness or accident had happened to me.

That was only human grace, so you can imagine what divine grace must be like.

Grace is God's Part: Faith is Man's!

If you had a present for someone you loved and he kept trying to do something to earn it, you'd feel rebuffed in your effort to show your unreserved affection. If you wanted him to work for the present, then it wouldn't really be a gift—it would be a wage.

That's what Paul says about man's efforts to work for God's favor: "Now to the one who works, his wage is not reckoned according to grace, but according to what is due. But to the one who does not work, but *believes* in Him [Jesus] who declares righteous the ungodly, his *faith* is reckoned as righteousness" (Romans 4:4, 5 paraphrased).

Nothing could be more clear.

A man's *faith* in what Jesus freely made available to him at the cross by *grace* is what God credits to his account as righteousness. I put my faith in Jesus, and He puts His righteousness into me.

Yeah, But ... !

The "cart-before-the-horse-crowd" is probably bursting right now with "Yeah, but what about the Book of James that says that 'faith without works is dead'?"

There's one thing for sure: if James means that faith and works *together* constitute salvation (as some believe he means), then his teaching is in diametric opposition to everything Paul taught. Now, since I don't believe the Bible can contradict itself, let's take a good look at what James was really emphasizing in the second chapter of his book.

The Man From Missouri

In chapter two, James is addressing a group of people who claim to be true believers in Jesus but don't manifest any evidence of this fact in their lives. So James takes the position that faith can only be seen *by men,* through what it produces in a life. He gives two completely different biblical case histories to prove this

point and to show that *true* faith always produces
evidence of its genuineness.

Case No. 1: Abraham

The first case James mentions is that of Abraham when
God called upon him to be willing to offer up his dearly
loved and only son, Isaac, as a sacrifice to the Lord. In
complete obedience and trust that God knew what He
was doing, Abraham actually went so far as to place
Isaac onto an altar and raise a knife above him to
plunge it into his heart. But God told Abraham to stop,
just in time. God saw what He wanted to see, and it
was that Abraham was still a man who would trust God
no matter what the case might be and that he was the
kind of man God could use to be the father of a race of
people called the "Hebrews."

You see, it's very important to note that this testing
in Abraham's life, recorded in Genesis 22, happened
forty years *after* God had already declared Abraham
righteous on the basis of his faith alone. Genesis 15:6
records the conversation that God initially had with
Abraham when He told him that he would have many
descendants. Abraham was about seventy-five years
old then, and he was childless. Even though he couldn't
figure out how he could be the father of so many
nations, he simply believed that if God said he would,
then he would.

And it was this simple faith in God that, alone,
caused God to count Abraham as righteous. From that
day, until the day that he actually took his son to
Mount Moriah to offer him as a sacrifice, nearly forty
years transpired, and many times during that period
Abraham failed God. But one thing stood sure in all
those years: he was still considered a righteous man by
God on the basis of his believing faith at the beginning.

After giving this illustration of Abraham's faith in
offering up Isaac, James says about this, *"You see* that
a man is justified by works, and not by faith alone"
(2:24).

It's true that *man sees* the works. But it's also true

that *God saw* Abraham's faith forty years before and on that basis pronounced him unconditionally righteous (Genesis 15; Romans 4:1-5).

The point is that after forty years of being righteous one should expect Abraham to show some evidence of his faith—and he did. But faith was the *means* of his salvation, and works were simply the *evidence* of the genuineness of it.

True faith will always produce works as evidence. But works will never produce true faith. Get the point?

Case No. 2: Rahab the Harlot

Lest we get the idea that in order to be declared righteous by God we must have some enormous demonstration of faith as Abraham did, James gives another case history to show how little a thing is evidence enough to show true faith.

At a time in Israel's history when she was seeking to enter the promised land, spies were sent from the wandering nation of Israel into Jericho to see what kind of opposition they would encounter if they tried to enter. Two Hebrew spies entered the home of a harlot named Rahab, and although she was a gentile and didn't know these two men, she hid them from her fellow countrymen when they came looking for the spies (Joshua 2:1-7).

After their pursuers were gone, Rahab told the Hebrew spies that her whole nation had heard about the Red Sea opening up for them forty years earlier. And how all the people of Jericho had lived in fear of the nation of Israel because of the great things their God had done for them in bringing them out of captivity in Egypt.

Then this gentile prostitute said, ". . . for the LORD your God, He is God in heaven above and on earth beneath. Now therefore, please swear to me by the LORD, since I have dealt kindly with you, that you also will deal kindly with my father's household" when you come in to conquer the land (Joshua 2:11, 12).

Now, this doesn't seem like much of a work, but it

was enough to show that she had come to believe in the God of Israel and that *belief* prompted her *act* of hiding Israel's spies.

From both these illustrations of James it can be seen that faith is only as good as its object, and the object must be God and confidence in His power and His word. When whatever faith we have, whether it be great like Abraham's or small like Rahab's, is placed in God then there will be the resulting evidence in our lives.

If there are never any righteous works in a person's life, then it well may be that there is no true faith. But if there is true faith, I guarantee you there will be good deeds eventually.

Faith, Plus Repentance?

Anytime anything is added to the one necessary ingredient of "faith" in order to receive God's salvation, then we're in danger of getting that cart in front of the horse again. Some people put a big stress on repentance as a necessary condition for receiving reconciliation. To be sure, repentance is definitely involved in becoming a child of God, but it must be carefully defined.

There are those who, in their zeal to get people to turn from their sinful ways and receive the Lord, almost put repentance on a par with believing. Repentance is defined by them as a deep sorrow over sin, usually evidenced by weeping and much emotion.

This is a faulty understanding of the word "repentance." It's certainly all right to have a deep emotional sorrow about having spent a life rejecting Christ, but that's not all that's involved in repentance.

Judas Iscariot felt such sorrow about betraying Jesus that he wept uncontrollably and even returned the money he'd received for turning Him over to His enemies. But he never repented or believed. Instead, he hung himself as a result of utter despair from guilt (see Matthew 27:3-5).

When we're talking with someone about his need for

Christ, we need to find out where his head is about the matter of sin. If he doesn't realize that he's a sinner, then he won't know that he needs a Savior. So in a case like that it might be necessary to emphasize God's view of sin and seek to show the person that according to the Bible's definition, he qualifies as a sinner.

But generally speaking, the emphasis should *not* be upon the man's personal sins—such as lying, cheating, adultery, dope, or what have you—with an effort to try to get him to feel bad for doing those things. The emphasis should be upon what God has done to remove *all* the barriers that separate God and man, including the barrier of sin. Jesus should be made the issue.

To Change, or Not to Change!
That's the Question!

The word repentance, *metanoeo* in the Greek, means to have a *change of mind* toward something or someone. It means a turning around from one attitude to another which produces a change in direction. It's a word related to our reason, rather than to our emotions, although whatever deeply affects our reason will also touch our emotions.

Repentance, as it relates to Christ, means to change our minds about Him, who He is and what He's done to provide forgiveness and deliverance from our sins. When we place faith in Jesus as having taken our place personally on the cross and borne the penalty due our sins, then we're automatically repenting, because we couldn't accept Him in this way without having had to change our minds in some way concerning Him.

The essence of the issue is this: you can repent and not believe; but you can't believe and not repent. This is why in the gospel of John, which was expressly written to bring people to new life in Christ, the condition "believe in Christ" is stated ninety-nine times. But the word "repent" isn't used at all in the book.

You may wonder why I've made an issue of this. It's

because I've seen people sit in a meeting or read a book about Christ's work of salvation for them, and they've said to themselves, "This is really true and I believe it," but then because they didn't have some deep emotional experience of repenting and getting all worked up, they haven't been sure whether their belief was sincere enough to save them.

Let me tell you right now, if while you've been reading this book, you've said to yourself, "This is true and I believe it. I don't understand it all, but I believe what I do understand," then I guarantee you that you've become a child of God. Whether your faith is strong like Abraham's or weak like Rahab's, it makes no difference. You've placed it in the right object by putting it in Christ.

Faith, Plus the Lordship of Christ?

This is a very subtle form of human merit which some add to "faith" as a condition of salvation. It's another "cart before the horse" and this one presents a tremendous problem, because it's an open-ended, indefinable condition.

For instance, who can say at this moment, no matter how long he's been a believer, that he has *everything* in his life under the lordship of Jesus? Most believers would like to have that be true, but as long as we're still in this world, with our unreformed sin natures, and the world, the flesh, and the devil are still out to get us, there's not much chance that there'll be a time in our lives when *everything* is under Christ's lordship at the same time.

If even mature believers are conscious of areas of their lives that aren't always in total submission to Christ, how can we make an unbeliever responsible to do something as a condition of salvation that we're still not able to do?

Those who say, "If Christ is not Lord of all, He's not Lord at all" have an admirable slogan, but they're laying a burden on the potential believer that's impossible to bear. But worse than that, they're subtly adding "works" to faith which nullifies grace and makes salvation, if not impossible, then very much of an albatross around the prospective believer's neck.

The scriptural teaching on this issue is that we must recognize Jesus as Lord in the sense that He's not a mere man, but the Lord from heaven who became a man to die for our sins. Yet even this understanding doesn't fully come until we've believed in Him as Savior and received new spiritual life so that we have the facility for understanding spiritual truth.

There's nothing wrong with telling an interested seeker that Christ wants to be his Lord once He comes to live within him, but unless that information is coupled with the teaching regarding the Holy Spirit's indwelling power to progressively make Jesus Lord of your life, then it's better not to bring it up. Once the person is saved, the Holy Spirit Himself will bring up the issue of Christ's Lordship.

In Romans 10:9, 10 Paul says this about what's involved in being saved, "If you confess with your mouth Jesus as Lord, and believe in your heart that God raised Him from the dead, you shall be saved; for with the heart man believes, resulting in righteousness, and with the mouth he confesses, resulting in salvation."

Two ingredients of salvation are mentioned in these verses. One is a *cause* and the other is an *effect*. One has to do with the heart or mind, and the other has to do with the mouth.

Look at the verses carefully. Paul says that what a man believes with his heart about Christ's resurrection and what it means will result in God giving him Christ's righteousness. That's another way of saying that the man has just become a child of God.

Then it says that with the mouth he is to confess or tell the world that Christ is the Lord and now his own personal Savior as well.

The believing is the *cause* of salvation, and the *effect* is the confession of Jesus as the Lord.

Faith, Plus Baptism?

The adding of a God-ordained ritual to faith as a condition of salvation down through the dark history of God's dealing with man has been one of the most subtle errors. The issue of water baptism has been the most confusing, since Jesus Himself commanded this ritual (Matthew 28:19, 20) and the Book of Acts shows that this was the common practice of believers.

There's no question but that a believer who's had the real meaning of water baptism explained to him will want to be baptized after receiving Christ as Savior. The rite of baptism is the believer's testimony to the world that he believes he's been totally identified with Christ in His death and burial, and he's now raised with Jesus into a new life where sin has no right to rule over him.

It's been particularly thrilling to me to see the way thousands of people today have desired to express in this dramatic, tangible way the fact that they have come to believe in Christ as their Savior. No one has laid any big trip on these people about the necessity of being baptized, but strangely enough, once they've been joined to Christ they just seem to want to jump into the nearest ocean, lake, or swimming pool and publicly announce that they belong to Christ.

But as beautiful and as meaningful as this necessary symbol is, it still must be seen as a *result* of salvation, not a *cause* of it, or even a partial cause of it. If we add baptism as a condition of being saved, then it becomes a work and an act of human merit which nullifies pure grace that says that nothing is needed from man, but faith.

An Old Error, Revived

The Jews at the time of Jesus, for the most part, made the same error as some believers do today. The ritual of circumcision given to them through Abraham corresponded to the ritual of water baptism today.

This teaching of the necessity of adding circumcision

to faith was the source of a great controversy in the early church (see Acts 15:1-11). The Apostle Paul, in demonstrating that salvation has always been by faith alone, selected two of the greatest men in the Old Testament as an illustration of that fact: Abraham and David.

Read carefully what Paul says of Abraham: "If Abraham was justified by works, he has something to boast about; but not before God. For what does the Scripture say? 'And Abraham *believed* God, and it was reckoned to him as righteousness' " (Romans 4:2, 3).

Then Paul shows that Abraham's being declared righteous before God on the basis of faith was apart from any ritual: "Is this blessing then upon the circumcised, or upon the uncircumcised also? For we say, 'Faith was reckoned to Abraham as righteousness.'

"How then was it reckoned? While he was circumcised, or uncircumcised?" And then Paul answers his own question, "Not while circumcised, but while uncircumcised; and he received the sign of circumcision, a seal of the righteousness of the faith which he had while uncircumcised" (Romans 4:9-11).

Paul argues relentlessly on this point, because any ritual, be it circumcision, Communion, or baptism, added to faith as a condition of salvation becomes a work of human merit, and that's incompatible with grace.

Paul Wasn't Sent to Baptize

Paul shows that baptism clearly isn't a condition of salvation when he says, "I thank God that I baptized none of you, except Crispus and Gaius, that no man should say you were baptized in my name."

And then he suddenly remembers some others he'd baptized and so he adds, "Now I did baptize also the household of Stephanas; beyond that, I do not know whether I baptized any other. For Christ did not send me to baptize, but to preach the gospel, not in cleverness of speech, that the cross of Christ should not be made void" (1 Corinthians 1:14-17).

Though Paul had led most of the Corinthian church to Christ, he couldn't remember too well whom he had baptized. Then he makes a colossal statement, "Christ didn't send me to baptize, but to preach the gospel." Paul's mission in life was to bring people into the salvation of Jesus Christ. If baptism were an integral part of the qualification for salvation, then he could never have made the above statement. Paul would have practically pulled a portable baptistry around behind him if baptism was a condition of the Gospel he was commissioned by Christ to preach.

Instead Paul concentrated on the one thing, preaching the Gospel. Because when men believe it, it's the power of God that brings salvation (see Romans 1:16, 17).

The Real Issue is Faith, Plus Nothing!

God has always had only one way of saving men, and that's been on the principle of "grace, through faith, not as a result of works, lest any one should have a reason to boast" about how he helped God save him (see Ephesians 2:8, 9).

Even in the Old Testament, salvation was by "Grace, through faith." There was no man who could say he deserved God's forgiveness. All men deserved His condemnation, but before Christ came, God graciously provided the animal sacrifices to picture the coming Lamb of God who would take away the world's sins.

However, simply offering sacrifices didn't save a man. He had to come in faith, believing that this was God's provision at that time to atone for his sins, and he had to trust in God to graciously withhold his judgment from him as long as he brought his offerings in faith.

The New Testament also clearly teaches that faith is the *means* of salvation. There are many *results*. Among them will be good deeds, repentance, Christ progressively becoming the Lord of your life, baptism, obedience, service, the fruits of the Spirit, spiritual gifts, and on and on.

But the issue that must remain central is that faith alone is all that's necessary for salvation. Remember the thief on the cross beside Jesus. He believed in Christ while hanging there in the process of dying. He couldn't come down from the cross and do any good deeds, he couldn't be baptized, and he couldn't go out and manifest the Christian life to the world by holy living.

Nevertheless, Jesus told him that that very day he would be in paradise with him because he had believed on Jesus.

I'm aware of the fact that some teach that God has had different ways of saving man at different times in human history. But if God ever compromised and made an exceptional case out of even one man's salvation, He would be honorbound by His own character to do it for all.

God's attribute of justice demands that He be equitable and fair with everyone, for as Paul points out in Romans 2:11, "there is no partiality with God." If God could save a thief by faith alone—and He did—then He must do it the same way for everyone.

Besides all this, if there had been some other way for man to be reconciled to God without God's having to put to death His dear Son, don't you think God would have done it? But that death was necessary to remove every barrier that stood between God and man so that God could deal with us in grace. Having done that, God isn't going to impose conditions on us for salvation which involve any human merit, thus nullifying what cost Him an infinite price to make a free gift to us.

Making Our "Withdrawal"

I said at the beginning of this chapter that if someone had put $100,000 in a bank account for you, it would do you no good unless you knew about it and then withdrew it from the bank.

Now you know what it is that God has done for you on the cross and how to draw upon it by faith alone.

The next move is up to you!

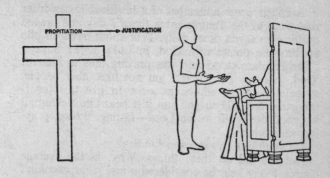

PROPITIATION ─────▶ JUSTIFICATION

Chapter Fourteen
Justification

There's a story in the New Testament which so beautifully illustrates justification that I'm going to begin with
it and wait a few pages even to define the word. By the
time you've digested this "Saga of Justification," little
definition will be necessary.

A Clergyman and a Tax Collector
(Luke 18:9-14)

Two men went over to the Temple to pray. One was a
super-religious do-gooder called a Pharisee, and the
other a tax collector, called a Publican.

A tax man in those days was considered by the
Pharisees, the religious crowd, to be the most wicked
sinner in the world. He was a man who betrayed his
own countrymen by collecting more taxes than were
assigned by the government. This dishonest profit was
the only payment for services he received; he didn't
get a salary. He was told to keep everything "over
and above." A Publican, then, made his money by
extortion from his fellow citizens.

A Pharisee was a member of a Jewish religious order
that went to the Temple three times a day and prayed
on his own seven times daily. Talk about trying to pile
up brownie points with God, in Luke 18:11 it says,
"The Pharisee stood and was praying thus to himself,
'God, I thank Thee that I am not like other people,
swindlers, unjust, adulterers, or even like this [*ugh*!]
tax-gatherer.' " Then you can just hear him ticking all
his good deeds off to the Lord—fasting, tithing, praying, sacrificing.

Do you think this guy was kidding?

No! He did all these things. Why, in the average
church today he'd be considered a real pillar, wouldn't
he? People would applaud him: "Look at this great
saint of God." Everything he did in the public eye was
beyond reproach.

Then in verse 13, the other man prayed, "God, be
merciful to me, the sinner." It says he was unwilling
even to lift his eyes to heaven, but instead was beating
his breast. This "beating of the breast" was a sign of
sorrow and unworthiness. He counted himself unworthy to come to God. His prayer reflected that.

Let's look more carefully at this prayer for mercy.

The Greek word *hilastheti* used here should *never*
have been translated into the English word "merciful"
because it actually means "to be propitious." I'm sure
that the translators felt the word "merciful" was a
more familiar word to the English reader than the word
"propitious," but theologically it does not connote the
true meaning of the word or the passage.

You see, God has never had to be persuaded to be
merciful. It was His mercy that caused Him to find a
way to satisfy His outraged holiness so that He could
act toward us in grace. When the tax-collector prayed
to God and asked Him to be "propitious" toward him,
he was actually saying, "I know you're not satisfied
with *me*. I'm nothing but a no-good sinner who only
deserves Your righteous wrath. But please receive me
in the light of the atoning blood of sacrifice on the
mercy seat which has satisfied your judgment against
me."

He may not have used those words, but when he asked God to be propitious toward him, that's exactly what he meant.

Jesus Looks at the Heart

What did Jesus say about this tax-collecting sinner?

"I tell you, this man went down to his house *justified* rather than the other; for everyone who exalts himself shall be humbled, but he who humbles himself shall be exalted."

To be humble means to have a true estimation of yourself and where you stand with God. To recognize there's nothing you can do to gain acceptance in God's sight, but to merely allow Him to make you acceptable.

By contrast, look at how the Pharisee approached God. He was full of pride about all the things he was *doing* to gain God's approbation. His deeds in themselves were not wrong, only his motives. His pride gave away the fact that he didn't understand the real meaning of God's propitiation through sacrifice.

Justification Defined

A simple definition which I've often heard defining "justification" is *"just-as-if-I'd* never sinned." It makes a clever-sounding phrase, but unfortunately it isn't correct.

You see, even in light of the fact that Christ has taken all my sins away, that only leaves me in a *neutral* status with God. Just having no sin will never make me acceptable in God's sight.

In order to be acceptable to God, I need more than just the *subtraction* of my sins. I need the *addition* of Christ's righteousness.

The Apostle Paul tells us how God arranged for this exchange. "God made Christ who knew no sin to be sin on our behalf, that we might become the righteousness of God in Him" (2 Corinthians 5:21). In other words, God took our sins and put them on Christ and then took Christ's righteousness and gave it to us in exchange.

That's what it means to be justified.

Because of the propitiation accomplished by Christ, God is now set free to instantly and irrevocably "declare righteous" any man, woman, or child who places faith in Christ as Savior. God declares that person to be just as righteous in *His* sight as His Son, Jesus Christ. This is our new "standing" with God.

The "Misinterpretation" That Split the Church

It's very important however, that the meaning of the word "justify" as used in the New Testament be precisely understood. There's a vast difference between being "declared" righteous by God and actually "becoming" righteous in my daily behavior. The first happens instantly the moment I believe in Christ and forever settles my acceptance and standing in the eyes of God. He can never again see me in any way except as having the righteousness of His Son.

However, my "becoming" righteous in my daily behavior is a life-long process which begins with my becoming a child of God, and it is culminated with my becoming just like Jesus the day I enter His eternal presence. But, whether I'm making good progress in my daily perfecting or not, it doesn't alter the fact that God continues to view me as absolutely righteous because of my union with Christ.

The biggest rift that ever developed in Christianity grew out of a confusion of this very issue of the difference between being "declared" righteous and actually "being" righteous in behavior. This rift became known as the "Reformation" and it forced a re-focus on two greatly abused truths: *first*, that justification is exclusively a work of God whereby He imparts to a believing soul the irrevocable righteousness of Christ; and *second*, Christ's righteousness is received by man at the *moment* of salvation on the basis of faith alone.

Luther and the Reformation of the Church

The German monk, Martin Luther, was the catalyst
that brought about the Reformation. The theology of
his day taught that justification meant that when one
professed belief in Christ, God declared all his *past*
sins forgiven. But he must then enter into a life-long
process of obtaining continued forgiveness and righteousness by his own religious performance. This
included the necessity of such things as good works,
self-denial, penance in the form of self-inflicted punishment and pain, prayers, confession, giving of money,
worship, and so forth.

In spite of careful performance of all these things,
Luther wrestled continually with a sense of spiritual
inadequacy. Finally, in desperation he determined to
go to Rome, the center of the Christian faith, and perform an act of penance and pain which might ease his
troubled conscience. While crawling on his knees up
the steps of a church in Rome, and wondering if all
this would bring him the sense of spiritual peace which
he sought, a verse from the Book of Romans kept
flashing across his mind: "The just shall live by *faith*"
(Romans 1:17, KJV).

There was no way Luther could equate what he was
doing at that moment with living by faith. He was
living by "works" and seeking to improve his righteousness in God's eyes by all these human merits.

In that instant the Reformation, which had been in a
long incubation period, was born. Luther got up from
his knees and with pen and preaching began to liberate
hundreds of thousands of sincere believers in God who
had never heard that Christ's death secured for them a
permanent and *total* forgiveness and righteous standing
with God which was obtainable *in toto* by faith in
Christ alone.

Justification by Faith: a Neglected Doctrine

Down through the dark history of the church, this fact
of "justification by faith" has been the most maligned,

misunderstood, and neglected truth of the Christian
faith. A failure to properly understand and accept the
reality of having been declared irrevocably righteous
by God has stripped believers of the assurance of their
standing with God and has crippled them into thinking
they must be on an endless treadmill of works in order
to maintain their acceptance with God.

It's hard to see how this vital truth could be missed
by anyone who's seeking to carefully examine and
teach the Word, since it's the heart of the message of
the Apostle Paul. What Jesus had introduced in numerous parables in the gospels concerning justification,
Paul amplified doctrinally in the epistles, particularly
in Romans and Galatians.

Obviously the reason Paul made such an emphasis
upon this truth is because of the impact that this
doctrine had upon his own life. He makes this clear in
his word of caution to the Philippians. In that letter to
this young church, Paul seeks to undo some of the
erroneous teaching that a group of super-religious
Pharisaical Jews had sown behind his back and which
subtly contradicted his previous teaching.

These Judaizers were Jews who in some ways accepted Jesus as the Messiah, but believed it was still
imperative to keep all the old Mosaic laws, as well as
being circumcised, if they truly wanted to be acceptable to God. This was diametrically opposed to what
Paul had taught. His emphasis was upon faith alone as
being sufficient to bring about salvation.

In his admonishment to the church in Philippians
3:1-9, Paul argues that the truly circumcised person is
the one who worships God in the Spirit and puts *no*
confidence in fleshly rituals or deeds. He then cites his
own admirable testimony of how blameless he was in
his keeping of the Jewish laws and his zealous persecu-
tion of the church, prior to his conversion.

Here's what he says: "If anyone else has a mind to
put confidence in the flesh, I far more: circumcised the
eighth day, of the nation of Israel, of the tribe of
Benjamin, a Hebrew of Hebrews; as to the Law, a
Pharisee; as to zeal, a persecutor of the church; . . ."

Now, notice what he says about his "law-keeping": ". . . as to the righteousness which is in the Law, *found blameless*" (Philippians 3:4b-6).

Two Kinds of Righteousness

You can see from what Paul just said that there are *two* kinds of righteousness. We've already discussed the first one, that which belongs exclusively to Christ and is imputed or credited to the one who does nothing more than place faith in Christ's atoning death. But the second kind of righteousness is that which comes out of an attempt to keep God's laws. This is strictly relative. In other words, God's perfect righteousness might be looked at as a standard representing 100 percent. All human efforts to keep God's laws measure somewhere from zero to one hundred, with *no one* reaching 100 percent.

As men look at our law-keeping, they applaud enthusiastically the closer we get to 100 percent, and usually we pat ourselves on the back. But from God's perspective, *anything* less than 100 percent perfect law-keeping flunks. That's what Isaiah meant when he said, "All *our* righteousnesses are as filthy rags in God's sight" (see Isaiah 64:6).

You've heard the saying, "The enemy of the best is the good." Nowhere is that more true than in this matter of righteousness. Although Paul could brag more than any Pharisee about how righteous he was in relation to keeping the Mosaic law, look at his estimation of the value of his own righteousness as over against that which he received from Christ. He says, "I count all things [*all those humanly produced good deeds*] to be *loss* in view of the surpassing value of knowing Christ Jesus my Lord, for whom I have suffered the loss of all things, and count them but rubbish in order that I may gain Christ, and may be found in Him, *not having a righteousness of my own derived from the Law, but that which is through faith in Christ, the righteousness which comes from God on the basis of faith*" (Philippians 3:8, 9).

The point of all Paul's trying to say here is that he was willing to compare his life with anyone who said his personal righteousness was enough to gain him God's acceptance, but if Paul's righteousness didn't save him, then no one else's law-keeping would save them either.

Why Israel "Missed the Ball"

In his letter to the Romans, Paul tells why the majority of the nation of Israel stubbornly clung to the wrong kind of righteousness and thereby missed out on God's salvation. "But Israel, pursuing a law of righteousness, did not arrive at that law. Why? Because they did not pursue it by *faith*, but as though it were by *works*. They stumbled over THE STUMBLING-STONE [*Jesus*]" (Romans 9:31, 32).

He further comments, "For I bear them witness that they have a zeal for God, but not in accordance with knowledge. For not knowing about God's righteousness, and seeking to establish their own, they did not subject themselves to the righteousness of God. For Christ is the end of the law for righteousness to everyone who believes" (Romans 10:2-4).

Paul wasn't just picking on his fellow Jews here. His heart's desire and constant prayer to God were for their eyes to be opened to see the mistake they were making by rejecting God's way to be made righteous and trusting in their own righteousness instead.

I'm Justified — So What?

I've used a lot of pages so far in this chapter to say two things over and over.

First, on the basis of Christ's propitiatory work on the cross, God's offended character has been satisfied and God is now free to impart a new dimension to all who receive His Son as Savior. This new dimension is the *righteousness of Christ* and it's like a cloak placed around a person, completely covering what he is in his own humanness, giving him a completely new standing in the eyes of God. This imputed righteousness means that every time God looks at me, now that I'm His child, He doesn't see my own righteousness (which falls far short of His perfection anyway); He sees me through the grid of Jesus' righteousness, and therefore I'm as acceptable to Him as His Son Jesus is, regardless of my daily performance.

The *second* point I've stressed is that this righteousness is given to a person, free and complete, the moment he places faith in Christ as Savior. It can't be added to, improved upon by God or man or ever revoked. It's given strictly on the basis of faith alone.

The ramifications in the life of the believer of "justification by faith" are incredible. We'll focus on the three major benefits: peace with God, a standing in grace, and no more condemnation.

Peace With God

In Romans 5:1 the Apostle Paul says, "Therefore having been justified by faith, we have *peace with God* through our Lord Jesus Christ."

"Having been justified" is in the aorist verb tense in the original Greek New Testament. This means it happened at a point of time in the past, and the implication here is that it never need be repeated because its effects go on forever.

It's imperative that once and for all we get straight in our minds the fact that we *have been* justified. If we don't, it's impossible to experience "peace with God." If I think my relationship with God is in constant jeopardy because of my failure to always live the Christian life correctly, then I'll be a nervous wreck, wondering whether God is upset with my performance. I can never experience peace with God until I begin to count as true the fact that I have been given Christ's righteousness and that makes me acceptable with God.

In their book, *Guilt and Freedom*,[1] Bruce Narramore and Bill Counts point out the hidden dangers of

---

[1] Bruce Narramore and Bill Counts, *Guilt and Freedom* (Santa Ana, Calif.: Vision House Publishers, 1974).

not seeing ourselves as God sees us. They correctly show that sin erected very real barriers between God and man and that although Christ has torn down the barriers and enabled God to reconcile men to Himself, there remain psychological barriers on the part of man. Man's knowledge of his failure to please God has brought fear of punishment, fear of rejection, and a loss of self-esteem.

There is absolutely no way to have these psychological barriers removed between ourselves and God until we accept as true the fact that God is now at peace with us because He has justified us once and for all. If I'm the least bit fuzzy in my thinking about this, then in spite of myself, I'm going to live with fear of punishment and rejection by God each time I fail Him. Eventually my sense of guilt will pile up so heavy on my head that I'll look at myself as a worm and of absolutely no worth to God.

Maybe you've never thought of it this way, but to have those kinds of feelings about yourself is like a slap in the face to Jesus. In essence, what you're saying when you fail to believe that you're totally acceptable to Him, just like you are, because of Christ's righteousness in you, is that you have higher standards for yourself than God does. And that attitude is both conceited and false.

If God says He is at peace with *us* on the basis of our justification, then what right do we have not to be at peace with God?

Peace With Ourselves and Others

One thing that's sure. If you don't have peace with God, then it will be impossible to be at peace consistently with yourself. You'll be constantly 'condemning yourself for your failures, and that self-condemnation will keep your focus on yourself instead of on Jesus and what He's done to remove God's wrath from you.

It's also impossible to be at peace with others if you haven't first settled in your mind that God is at peace

with you. The last great commandment Jesus gave to
His disciples was "Love one another, in the same way
as I have loved you" (John 13:34). If you're not convinced that God's love for you is unconditional on the
basis of His justification of you, then your love for
others won't be unconditional either. You'll accept
them in the same way that you see yourself accepted by
God. That is, when you perform up to God's expectations, He accepts you; when you don't perform, He
doesn't.

That's the way you'll respond to those around you.
When they meet your expectations, you'll give them
unconditional acceptance. When they let you down,
you'll withdraw your full acceptance of them until they
shape up and start performing up to your standards
again.

All this fouled-up thinking is straightened out by
simply believing that what God says is true of us, is
true. We *have been* justified and now God is at peace
with us and nothing will ever cause Him to stop being
at peace with us.

The only issue is, will we believe what He says
about our justification and be at peace with him?

A Standing in Grace

A second great benefit which has come to the believer
through justification by faith is a new standing in grace.

"Therefore having been justified by faith, we have
peace with God through our Lord Jesus Christ, through
whom also we have obtained our introduction by faith
into this *grace in which we stand*" (Romans 5:1, 2).

Remember that we defined grace as being "all that
God has set Himself free to give us and do for us completely apart from any human merit." If we can earn it
in any way, then it can't be given to us on the basis of
grace.

Paul tells us in this passage in Romans that we have
a standing in grace. This means God can treat us in no
other way than by grace because that's our new stand-

ing with Him. There'll never be a time in our lives when God will require us to deserve or earn any blessing or favor from Him.

I don't know why it's so hard for people to really believe this. They can accept the fact that they could do nothing to deserve or earn their initial salvation, but somehow they've gotten the idea they must earn the right to be used by God or have His blessings once they've become His child.

I found myself subtly slipping into this thinking only recently. Jan and I were given a chance for a week's vacation on a cruise to Mexico. It was like a dream come true. We were waited-on hand and foot, the food was sensational, and best of all, there were no telephones ringing or appointments to keep. But about the third day out, I began to feel guilty about having such a good time. Jan sensed something was wrong and she asked me what it was. I told her I was feeling guilty because I felt I didn't really deserve to have the Lord give me such a bountiful display of His love.

Whereupon, Jan reminded me, "When did you ever *deserve* any of the blessings God has given you?"

That's really the truth! When did any of us ever deserve anything from a holy and righteous God except His wrath? And yet, because He has declared us as righteous as His Son, Jesus, God is able to give us His gracious blessings at any time, quite apart from any merit in us. It's because of our standing in grace with Him.

Relax, Believer!

One of the marvelous things about being in an atmosphere of grace is that you don't have to walk around on eggshells worrying about offending someone or getting someone uptight with you. I'm sure we've all known people who create anything but an atmosphere of grace, and the whole time we're around them we're watching our Ps and Qs to be sure we perform just right. It isn't long before that kind of relationship gets to be a drag and we don't want to be around the person.

This often becomes one of the major factors in marital problems. One of the partners has the other on such a performance-based relationship that if the other one doesn't always come across as the model mate, they really let them know that they've been displeased. Instead of freeing the offensive partner to become the ideal mate, it simply tightens him up worrying about whether he's just done something wrong or not. It definitely *isn't* an atmosphere of grace.

But with God we don't have to walk around on eggshells because we have a standing in grace with Him, and He just doesn't get bugged with us when we fail to perform the way He might want. You see, our acceptance with Him is based on one key factor only: we are in His Son and His Son's righteousness is in us.

That's what it means to be "accepted in the beloved" (Ephesians 1:6, KJV). Jesus is the Beloved, and since I'm in Him, and He's in me, I'm accepted by the Father in the same way He is.

No More Condemnation

The third, and yet perhaps least understood, benefit of justification is that God doesn't condemn us anymore. That's what Paul was talking about when he wrote, "There is therefore *now* no condemnation for those who are in Christ Jesus" (Romans 8:1).

Boy, do I ever remember the day that truth hit me. It exploded in my life like a bombshell. I was under such a pile of self-condemnation, and what I thought was God's condemnation, that I could hardly see out from under the pile.

I was just reading that verse one day, and all of a sudden I discovered the word "now." I don't know where it had been all that time, but I saw it for the first time and did it ever speak to me! I realized right then that on the basis of everything Paul had said in the first seven chapters of Romans about Jesus' death and resurrection, I wasn't under God's condemnation now and never could be again. That set the stage for me to stop condemning myself and stop believing

others who tried to make me feel guilty because I
wasn't living up to their ideas of what a Christian
ought to be.

The sheer magnitude of this "no condemnation"
concept has obviously been hard for the church to
handle all down through its history. You can't find
much written about it in early church writings because
it wasn't clearly taught or understood. Part of that
reason has to do with an incorrect addition to the text
of Romans 8:1. Let's take a look at it.

The Naked Truth of "No Condemnation"

In the first verse of Romans 8, where Paul makes the
summary statement that "there is therefore now no
condemnation for those who are in Christ Jesus," you'll
notice that the King James Version of the Bible adds a
further statement, "who walk not after the flesh, but
after the Spirit." This phrase is not in any of the
earliest Greek manuscripts dating before the fourth
century and was obviously added by someone or a
group of people sometime during the middle centuries
of the church. None of the most recent Bible transla-
tions include it.

It has been thought that the addition of this seemingly innocent and supposedly correct statement was
the mistake of some scribe who glanced at the end of
Romans 8:4, where this same phrase ends the verse,
and accidentally copied it onto verse one.

I personally don't see how that could have happened
because it's inconceivable to me that any one man
could have had such unsupervised liberty in copying
the most sacred document in the possession of the
church.

My personal opinion is that the naked truth of the
statement that Paul made—"there is therefore now
no condemnation for those who are in Christ Jesus"—
was simply more than some of the early church fathers
could handle. They were willing to grant that if we
walked in the Spirit we couldn't be condemned, but
they couldn't accept the fact that just being in Christ

and His righteousness being in us could make us free of all condemnation.

But, praise God, that's exactly what Paul meant to say because that's the truth!

If we'll just accept the statement for what it says and not bring our own religious bias to it, we can soon discover that Paul had good grounds on which to tell us that there's no more condemnation for us.

But before we look at those grounds, we need to define just what it means to no longer be condemned. There are two facets to the concept of "condemnation."

Condemned by Whom and for What?

First, there's the genuine reality of the fact that unless a person believes in the redemptive work of Christ on the cross, he *is* condemned to an eternal separation from God in a very real place called hell.

But once that person has believed in Christ's sub-stitutionary death in his place, Jesus Himself promised, "Truly, truly, I say to you, he who hears My word, and believes Him who sent Me, has eternal life, and *does not come into condemnation,* but has passed out of death into life" (John 5:24).

So the issue of *eternal* condemnation is a settled matter in the life of a true believer in Jesus. That's the very essence of what Jesus was saying. If we've passed from death into life, we can't go back into death again unless God undid His whole work of justification, and there's *NO* chance of that happening.

However, what's at stake in the misunderstanding of Romans 8:1 is whether, having been delivered from *eternal* condemnation, a believer can come back under any form of condemnation by God because of his be-havior.

The answer to that is an absolute NO.

The very reason that verse is located where it is, is meant to establish the finality of the fact that we can never again be condemned by God from the minute we believe in Jesus as Savior. In Romans 7 we see the picture of the believer, Paul, going through the most despairing period of his Christian life. It seems to Paul like everything is condemning him—the Law of God, his own conscience, and possibly, even God Himself.

But one chapter later in Romans 8, Paul is joyously writing of the fact that "If God be for us, who can be against us" (verse 31 KJV). This is no longer a defeated and despairing believer.

Now, what do you think it was that brought him out of the despair of Romans 7 and into the victory of Romans 8?

One great fact!

He realized there was no more condemnation from the Law, from God, and consequently no legitimate condemnation from his own conscience, because he was *in* Christ Jesus. And the realization of that set him free to begin to allow the indwelling Holy Spirit to make him holy in his daily living and to actually live in, and out through him, the very righteousness of Christ.

Realizing that he didn't have to live *for* God in order not to be condemned, he began to relax and trust the Holy Spirit to live the Christian life *through* him. That's what he meant when he said God rejected the method of using laws to try to make people behave the right way, because it never worked (Romans 8:3). But the same result of righteousness was achieved by walking in dependence upon the indwelling Holy Spirit and letting Him produce the righteousness of God *in* him (Romans 8:4).

The Grounds of "No Condemnation"

Now let's look at just a couple of the arguments Paul calls upon to substantiate the fact that God will *never* be the source of any condemnation of one of His children.

The first argument has a basis in the laws of jurisprudence which govern the courtrooms of America and other countries as well. There's a law called "the Law of Double Jeopardy." This law states that an individual cannot be subjected to a second trial and penalty for the same offense.

This has a perfect application in the case of God against man. God has already condemned Jesus *in our place* for every sin we will ever commit. For that reason, and true to the law of double jeopardy, He cannot and will not condemn the one who believes in Jesus as his substitute and Savior. One person has already taken our penalty. Now we don't have to.

Peter explains Jesus' taking our place in this way: "For Christ also died for sins once for all, the *just for the unjust,* in order that He might bring us to God" (1 Peter 3:18a). He was the "just" One and we were the "unjust."

God is on Our Side

Paul's second argument as to why we can never be condemned by God, once we become His children, reaches deep into the very character of God Himself. Two great facets of God's character, His sovereignty and His immutability (unchangeableness), are called upon to witness to the fact that God is unalterably "for us" and could never condemn us again.

In Romans 8:31-35 Paul sums up this second argument by posing five penetrating questions, the answers of which form a powerful argument for God never again condemning us and why neither we nor anyone else can legitimately condemn us either.

The first question: "If God is for us, who is against us?" (verse 31). The very nature of the question implies that "whoever" might be against us, they don't amount to anything because the Almighty, Sovereign God of the Universe is for us.

That fact can be mighty comforting when you've made your stand for the Lord in a hostile situation and you feel a little like the Lone Ranger. Joshua, the prophet of old, quoted God, "Have I not commanded you? Be strong and courageous! Do not tremble or be dismayed, for the LORD your God is with you wherever you go" (Joshua 1:9).

The second question: "He who did not spare His own Son, but delivered Him up for us all, how will He not also with Him freely give us all things?" (Romans 8:32). The point here is that if, when we were still enemies of God, He gave up the most precious thing He had in our behalf, now that we're His children, will He give us less? Of course not!

The "all things" He's promised to freely give us refer to the thousands of privileges and blessings outlined in the promises of God throughout the entire Bible. They're like a treasure storehouse just waiting to be entered.

You can see, on the basis of this unequivocal statement, that there's no need to beg at the back door of heaven for any of your needs. Paul wrote to the Philippians, "My God shall supply all your needs according to His riches in glory in Christ Jesus" (Philippians 4:19).

Part of the blessing of knowing we can never be condemned again is the certainty that when we go to the Lord in prayer, we'll find a gracious and loving acceptance no matter how we've been behaving in our Christian lives. You see, when we were His bitter enemies, He did the most for us, and He won't do less now that we're His children.

The third question: "Who can (is qualified to) bring a charge against God's elect?" (Romans 8:33). Who has a right to bring accusations or condemnations against a person who has been declared righteous by the sovereign Judge of the universe? The answer is, "Only the Judge Himself!" But will the Almighty Judge of Heaven do this? Paul doesn't even bother to answer the question with a No because the answer is so obvious. God is the One who justified man, so He's not about to declare man unjust and condemned again.

What it boils down to is that God can't reverse a sovereign, immutable declaration which He's already made, even if He wanted to. And since it cost God the most incredible price that He could pay to justify man, why would He now want to throw all that out and say it was all for nothing? There's no remote chance that He would. The cost was too great!

The fourth question: "Who was the one who condemns?" (Romans 8:34). There's a saying, "Don't

count your critics: weigh them!" That really applies
here. There may be ever so many people, including
yourself, who will condemn you, but there's only One
who has the *right* to, and that's Jesus Himself.

John tells us, "For not even the Father judges any
one but He has given all judgment to the Son, in order
that all may honor the Son, even as they honor the
Father" (John 5:22,23).

Now, the question is, will Jesus condemn the one
whom the Father has already declared righteous? We
must again answer with a resounding NO! To do so
would contradict four of His mightiest works in our
behalf.

The *first* was that "He died for us." The *second,*
"He was raised from the dead" to prove the Father's
acceptance of His atonement for us. *Thirdly,* "He sits
at God's right hand" as a glorified man assuring the
fact that we'll also be there one day. The *fourth* is that
He is continually "interceding for us" as our high priest
(see Romans 8:34).

The fifth question: "Who shall separate us from the
love of Christ?" (Romans 8:35). The question really
is, "Is there anything or anyone, anywhere in this
world or the spiritual realm, who can, by its condemnation, cause God's unchangeable love to stop flowing
toward us?" The point of all that Paul's said in Romans 8 is that there isn't.

Now, that's not to say there won't be those who *will*
condemn us and accuse us of having "fallen from God's
grace" because of some behavior which they've judged
as being wrong, and perhaps, really was wrong. But
nothing, not even wrong behavior, can ever cause
God to condemn one of His children again.

Because so few believers really understand the
depths of this truth, they mistake the condemnation of
Satan, fellow believers, and their own consciences as
being from God. Satan is called "the accuser of the
Brethren" by the Apostle John in Revelation 12:10.
He accuses believers because he knows he won't get
anywhere trying to accuse us before God. But if we
aren't anchored in the bedrock truth of the fact that

God can't and won't ever condemn us again, we may fall for Satan's accusations and actually think they're from God.

Since God No Longer Condemns, Do You?

Since God has gone to such great lengths to prove He doesn't condemn us anymore, then do we have a right to condemn ourselves? No one can have a bold faith when he's walking around condemning himself for his miserable performance as a child of God.

True faith comes from focusing on Christ and what He's done for you through justification. But if you don't concentrate on that and instead focus on your behavior as a believer, you'll soon end up being discouraged and condemning yourself for your failure to live up to what you know God requires of you.

It's also true that if you condemn yourself for a shabby Christian life, you're bound also to have a critical view of others. We hate most in others what we hate about ourselves. Yet if Christ doesn't condemn a brother, but accepts Him on the basis of having declared him righteous in Christ, then what right do I have to condemn him? As the Scriptures say, "Who are you to judge the servant of another? To his own master he stands or falls; and stand he will, for the Lord is able to make him stand" (Romans 14:4).

Whan an incredible promise! Don't we all know some Christian friend who hasn't been living very close to God and we've taken all kinds of "spiritual" potshots at him? This verse of Scripture should give great encouragement to us because it says he is God's servant and the Lord is able to make him stand. And stand he will!

It may be that *our* condemnation of him is the very thing keeping him from seeing that God is not condemning him for having strayed. Nobody wants to snuggle up to a porcupine, and if an erring believer thinks God is still angry with him and just waiting to condemn him, he'll never want to come back into fellowship with the Lord.

Our loving and accepting attitude may be his path back.

Justification is the Name of the Game

I realize that this chapter has been the longest one in the book, but how could I have hurried through this most critical truth of justification by faith? If we aren't straight in our thinking on this subject, nothing else will work right in our Christian lives.

In summing it up, let me say that justification is the work of God whereby He declares righteous, on the basis of faith alone, that one who simply believes in Jesus as Savior. This righteousness is something which is added to the believer when he believes and can never be taken away. It assures him of three great realities: peace with God, a standing in grace, and no more condemnation.

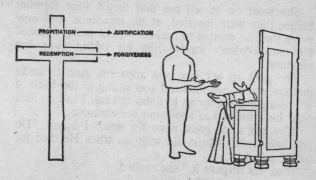

PROPITIATION ⟶ JUSTIFICATION

REDEMPTION ⟶ FORGIVENESS

Chapter Fifteen

Forgiveness

In beginning this chapter, let me say that some of you who have read my book, *Satan Is Alive and Well on Planet Earth,* will recognize some of this material from the chapter entitled "The Guilt Trip." In that volume I presented the subject of forgiveness from the standpoint of seeing more clearly our victory over Satan. Here I want to demonstrate the power of forgiveness from the standpoint of the total Christian life.

Not long ago I was speaking to a group of young married couples on the truths of the total forgiveness in Jesus Christ. A young gal stayed around until everyone else had gone and then walked up and said, "I have a question."

"All right," I said. "What can I do to help?"

She told me she and her husband were both believers, but they'd only been married about three months and were already having problems.

"I know this may sound stupid," she said, "but I can't forgive him because of something he did. And it was really as much my fault, I guess, as it was his."

She went on to tell me that they'd slept together before they were married, at his insistence, and now every time he wanted to make love, she really resented him and couldn't forgive him for taking away her virginity.

The guilt on her face was apparent. And to make matters worse, her husband was sitting at the back of the room, waiting for us to finish talking. I had no idea what his attitude was about our conversation.

"I've got some great news for you," I began. "Do you know what Christ did with sin when He died for us?" I asked.

"Yes, He forgave it," she replied.

"How much of it?" I asked.

"Everything."

"How many of yours and your husband's sins did Jesus forgive?" I said.

"All of them," she answered.

"Well then," I said, "if God has forgiven you and your husband, don't you think you should forgive yourself and him too?"

"I'd never really thought about it that way before," she said. "Praise the Lord, I really *do* forgive him."

She thanked me and was about to turn around and head over to where her husband was waiting.

"I hate to hold you up," I said. "But there's one more thing you ought to know."

The expression on her face looked as if she thought I was going to withdraw some of the good news I had told her and recant on it.

"The other thing is that God has not only forgiven you two, but *He has forgotten it's ever happened!* Because Hebrews 10:17 says, 'Their sins and their lawless deeds I will remember no more.' Not only has He forgiven you, but He's chosen not to remember it. Because of Christ's death on the cross, it's covered. Now, since He's forgotten all about it, you two forget it too. Okay?"

"Wow! Thank you," she said. "This is the greatest thing I've ever heard."

She took off like a bullet, ran across the room, and

hugged her hubby so hard it almost knocked him off his chair. Needless to say, that marriage was going to be different from then on because all unforgiveness ever produces is a sense of estrangement.

Redemption is the Ground of Forgiveness

Now, before anyone is tempted to protest that my counsel to her made a light thing out of a serious sin, let's see just how extensive God's forgiveness for sin really is.

As you can see from the diagram at the beginning of this chapter, forgiveness is one of the results of Christ's redemptive work on the cross. As we'll see in the next chapter, freedom is another. Man's debt of sin was canceled out by Christ's redemption, making it possible for God to totally forgive us all our sins. Then He purchased us out of the slave market of sin and gave us freedom.

In this chapter we concentrate on what it means to be forgiven by God.

In Colossians 2:13 Paul sets forth the extent of God's forgiveness in the clearest possible way. He speaks here to the young believers in the church at Colossae: "And when you were dead in your sins and the uncir-cumcision of your flesh, He made you alive together with Him, having forgiven us all our sins."

Three things are emphasized here. First, God says we were all dead in our sins at one time. This is the state of all of us before we came to Christ. We learned this in the chapter on spiritual death.

Second, God has made us alive in Christ. This is a fantastic truth, and we'll look at it carefully in chapter seventeen on regeneration.

Third—and this is the facet of this passage that we want to concentrate on here—"God has forgiven us all our sins." The verb "having forgiven" in Colossians 2:13 is in the aorist tense in the Greek, meaning it happened at a point of time in the past. In other words, once God dealt with sin at the cross, it was a closed case.

I want us to lock in on one particular phrase in this verse, "forgiven us *all* our sin."

Have you ever stopped to consider how much "all" really is? A lawyer friend of mine told me that in a legal decision stemming from a case in Pennsylvania, the word "all" was defined this way: "*All* includes everything and excludes nothing."

All Isn't Always All, to All

But you know, in the mind of the average Christian, when he reads the words "having forgiven us *all* our sins," he thinks it refers to all the sins he committed *before* he accepted Jesus. I used to think this.

Say that this diagram represents my life—

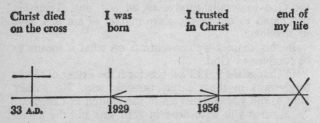

| Christ died on the cross | I was born | I trusted in Christ | end of my life |

33 A.D.   1929   1956

Up here to the left, Christ died for my sins in A.D. 33. Further on in history, a guy named Hal Lindsey was born in 1929. Then in 1956, he accepted Jesus Christ.

Okay—born, 1929, received Christ, 1956. I used to think that when I believed in Jesus Christ as my personal Savior, He forgave all my sins from the day I was born up until 1956, as a result of His death in A.D. 33. I don't know what I thought His provision was for the rest of my life! I guess I felt I had to somehow get forgiveness for all my future sins by confessing each one right after I did it.

But how many of my sins were future when Christ died? ALL OF THEM! Do you know that the sins I committed from 1956 until the day I go to be with Christ are just as much paid for as the previous ones? They were all so offensive to a holy God, that in A.D.

33 He *had* to deal with *everything* I would ever do wrong. In order for God to have forgiven me in 1956, He had to have forgiven me for all future sins *or He could not have accepted me in the first place!* You see, my future sins were as real and repugnant to God as my past ones.

Half a Cross Isn't Enough for Salvation

Many people have a concept of a cross that only looks to the rear of their lives, but never looks ahead. That's only half of a cross and that's really no cross at all. When God says He forgave us *all* our sins, that's a cross with two arms, one stretching back into our past and one reaching into our entire future. Anything less than an all-inclusive forgiveness on the timeline of history falls pathetically short of God's infinite provision for sin.

The Two Most Important Truths About Forgiveness

First, we saw in our chapter on redemption that when Christ went to the cross, He took there with Him the certificates of debt, listing *all* the sins of all mankind, and once and for all dealt with all sin by taking it out of the way as a barrier to God (Colossians 2:14).

Then in Hebrews 10:14 and 17 another facet of this great truth is added. By Christ's offering of Himself as our sacrifice, He has procured a forgiveness for us that's *eternal* and *irreversible.* Verse 17 says, "And their sins and their lawless deeds I will remember no more."

Isaiah the prophet quoted the Lord as saying the same thing: "I, even I, am the one who blots out your transgressions for My own sake; and I will not remember your sins" (Isaiah 43:25).

These two truths form the bedrock foundation that you must build on in order to experience the reality of God's forgiveness in your daily life.

First, all your sins—past, present, and future—were

forgiven when you believed in Jesus. There are none He hasn't already forgiven.

Second, not only has He forgiven you *all* your sins, but He's blotted them out from His own memory forever. They'll never be brought up against you again.

Can We Forgive as God Has?

If God has forgiven us all our sins and isn't holding them against us anymore, then what should our attitude be about sins in ourselves and others? Thousands of hospital beds, mental institutions, and jails are filled with people who have never forgiven themselves or others for wrongdoings. This kind of poison eats away at a person until real illness or damaging hostility results.

One of the key factors in unhappy marriages is the fact that two people living in such intimate proximity to each other see the worst there is in the other one. In this kind of emotionally charged relationship, while the rough edges are being worn off each other, things are often said and done that are unkind or cruel. If these things are allowed to fester and are never forgiven, bitterness and resentment can build up inside the two partners to the point where complete estrangement takes place.

More and more people take what they consider the easy "out" when this kind of alienation occurs: they get a divorce. But that hasn't really solved the problem of the lack of forgiveness in the person's heart. All they do is take it with them into their next marriages, and the new partners get punished with the inner hostility.

In many cases, marriages that appear to be fairly normal on the outside also suffer because there's unforgiveness on the part of one or both partners. They punish each other by sexual neglect, sloppy housekeeping and personal grooming, failure to achieve in their jobs, attention to others of the opposite sex, fighting, frigidity, constant criticism and nagging, and on and on. Both they and their children suffer from the lack of forgiveness.

There are also many people who have never been able to forgive themselves for their past sins. Maybe they've had a secret habit which they've felt was sin, and because they can't forgive themselves, they get a terrible self-image. They feel they're no good, and they develop a self-consciousness and inferiority complex.

Or, a knowledge of their inner sin-life causes some people to develop a defensiveness that makes them hostile and argumentative. It's as though they have the attitude that no matter how little they really think of themselves, they're going to be very sure no one else sees how raunchy they are inside.

Is All This Bitterness Necessary?

There's only one basis on which we can fully forgive ourselves and others for sins and shortcomings. We have to know and continually count on the reality of the complete forgiveness by God for those very same sins we've developed the bitterness over. If God isn't holding those things against us and He's forgiven and forgotten, then we can too!

Now, you might be thinking to yourself, "Yes, but if you only knew what he did to me, you'd see why I can't forgive him."

But you know, God could say that to us about what our sins did to His only, and dearly beloved Son, Jesus. They sent Him to the cross to suffer in a way that none of us could ever imagine. And yet, God has forgiven us, for Christ's sake.

For me to fail to forgive myself or anyone else who has offended me is to say that I have a higher standard of forgiveness than God, because whatever it is that has so hurt me that I can't forgive it, God already has.

The Sin Syndrome: Sin, Guilt, Estrangement

A failure to understand properly the full extent of God's forgiveness is always going to hamper our spiritual lives. It's because there's an inevitable cycle involved with sinning, even after we've become children of God.

When we sin, the Holy Spirit convicts us and we experience a bonafide conviction which is referred to in 2 Corinthians 7:8-11 as "godly sorrow." However, if that "sorrow" is not properly related to the forgiveness God procured at the cross, it will lead to guilt and that will lead to estrangement from God. This estrangement doesn't mean we don't belong to God anymore. But it can cause us to live in fear of God's punishment or rejecting us, and that leads to a sense of inferiority before God.

Now, how can this "sin syndrome" of sin, guilt, and estrangement be broken? We know we don't stop committing sins even though we're believers. So how can we keep from developing guilt which leads to estrangement from God?

Here's the solution. When I knowingly sin, I must confess my sin to the Lord (1 John 1:9). The word "confess" is a combination of two Greek words, *homo* and *logeo*. These two words together mean "to say the same thing about something that someone else says about it." In this case, when I've sinned, I must say the same thing about my sin that God says about it.

Now, what does God say about my sin?

First of all, He says it *is* sin. So I agree with God that what I just did was sin. I don't try to make excuses for myself or cover it up; I openly admit that I sinned. And if I know that I'm already forgiven, then I'm not afraid to come to God and be honest with Him about my sin.

Secondly, God says He *has* forgiven all my sins, including that one I just committed. So I look to the cross of Jesus and there remind myself of the great fact of my forever forgiveness which He purchased there. Then I thank Him that in His sight my sin has *already been* forgiven. Jesus has already suffered and died for the penalty of that sin.

And *thirdly,* out of appreciation for that great forgiveness, I accept it gratefully, turn from my sin, and begin to focus consciously upon the Lord Jesus again, drawing upon His Holy Spirit, who is indwelling me and who alone can empower me not to sin.

The Consequences of Not Relating Sin to the Cross

When a believer sins, he's immediately convicted by the Spirit. Even if he's hardened his heart through many ignorings of the Spirit's conviction, the Spirit can always be counted on to get through in that still, small voice. If the believer doesn't immediately relate that sin to the cross and the forgiveness that's already his because of it, then it will eventually produce a sense of guilt which is not from God. And that guilt will lead into a temporal estrangement from God.

Now, when we sin, a strange phenomenon sets in. We instinctively know that someone has to pay. Even if we don't recognize this on the conscious level, it occurs in our subconscious minds.

Since we can't cope with this unresolved inner conviction, we'll handle it in one of three ways. Either we'll punish ourselves in some way in an effort to make up for the sin, or we'll punish someone else. Or we'll look to the cross of Jesus and believe that He's already borne the punishment in such a permanent way that we have no need for personal recriminations or taking it out on anyone else.

Sin is No Longer the Issue

What I've been trying to say through this whole chapter is that there's no longer any reason to focus on sin in our lives. The work of Christ in redemption has so completely dealt with our sins that they can never be brought up against us again after we come to know Jesus as our personal Savior.

Now, you may be wondering: if sin is no longer an issue with God, what should my attitude be toward sin as I find it coming into my daily life?

First of all, as I already discussed, it should be confessed and God's forgiveness appropriated. But if there's some insensitivity to the Spirit's convicting, and we fail to agree with God that what we did was sin, then He'll keep putting His finger on the sin and make an issue of it until we admit it was sin and claim His forgiveness. If we fail to readily agree with God that we've sinned, when He's convicted us of it, then He may be forced to discipline us—but even that's always done in love, not anger (Hebrews 12:5-13).

The words "discipline" and "training" are interchangeable. God's disciplining is always forward looking, and that's why it's comparable to training.

When God sees a child of His who continually refuses to depend upon the Holy Spirit to deliver him from his temptations, out of deep concern for the child's well-being and happiness God will begin to train and discipline him so that he will come to depend upon Him in the future. God knows we're happy only when we're living holy lives.

But even when God has to discipline us, His focus is not so much on our sins as it is on the lessons He's teaching us about walking in dependence upon His indwelling Spirit.

I know it worries some people to hear that our sins are no longer an issue with God, beeause they wonder what will motivate people to keep in line if they aren't worried about God coming down on them for their sins.

Well, I can't find any verses of Scripture that ever sanction a child of God "worrying about his sins" as a proper motivation for serving and loving God. But there are abundant verses that teach us that God isn't alienated from us anymore now that we're His children and all He requires of us is to walk by faith so we won't fulfill the lusts of our sinful natures (Galatians 5:16).

It's easy to walk by faith when you *know* you're forgiven. You're not afraid to be honest with God if you *know* He isn't carrying a club, just waiting for you to sin so He can get even with you. You can't wait to love and serve a God whose *only* attitude toward you is one of love and complete acceptance.

Isn't it great to know you're forgiven?

Now, let the realization of this cause you to forgive yourself for that thing which you've been holding in your conscience. And let it also lead you to forgive those toward whom you've been harboring bitterness and unforgiveness.

That's the pathway to real freedom!

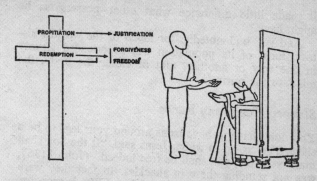

Chapter Sixteen
Freedom

If there's one word that expresses the battle cry of the decade of the 1960s, it's FREEDOM.

Those ten years witnessed the often frenzied efforts of millions to throw off their feeling of being shackled. Students wanted freedom in determining the courses they should be required to take, and who their teachers should be. Minorities wanted freedom from the exploitation and racism they had felt for centuries. Children wanted to be free from parental supervision and authority. Workers wanted more freedom in determining their working conditions. Churchgoers wanted freedom from the stifling and rigid form of institutional churches. Millions of Americans wanted our military forces to be free of involvement in Vietnam and any other war games.

In short, the 1960s saw the emergence of millions of "freedom freaks."

But I have an idea that long before the '60s the word "freedom" was the most cherished word in every language known to man. For if a man lost his freedom,

175

it made little difference what other possessions he might have.

And yet, undoubtedly, for much of the world's history, most of its population has experienced slavery in one way or another, that of either the body, the mind, or the spirit.

Slavery Has Many Faces

You don't have to have irons around your legs to be a slave. The crowd to whom Jesus said, "If the Son shall make you free, you shall be free indeed" (John 8:36), was not standing there in shackles. In fact they were the ruling elite of the nation of Israel. Their response to this straightforward rebuke showed how little they really realized their inner condition of heart: "We are Abraham's offspring, and have never yet been enslaved to any one; how is it that You say, 'You shall become free'?" (John 8:33).

Jesus went on to explain to them that their bondage was an inner one. They belonged to Satan.

In chapter five we saw that one of the barriers separating God and man was man's slavery to Satan. But man was also a slave to two other forces, the old sin nature and the Law, and he just as desperately needed to be set free from them as from Satan himself.

This chapter shows how the redemptive work of Christ on the cross unshackled mankind and allowed God to give us freedom from (1) the tyranny of our inborn natures of sin, (2) the principle of law with its demands for obedience or death, and (3) that sadistic slave master of men, Satan.

Twentieth-Century Allegory

There's a story the Apostle Paul tells in the first four verses of Romans 7 that more than anything else has helped me understand *how* I was set free from bondage to the sin nature, the Law, and Satan. Although the story, as I'm going to tell it, will be an "amplified" version of what Paul wrote, still, I believe, this is what he was really trying to say. This will be a twentieth-century interpretation.

Once upon a time there was a lovely, gentle woman who found herself married to a demanding, tyrannical perfectionist. All he did, from the day they were married, was lay down the law to her about how he wanted her to behave as his wife. Nothing was ever good enough for him no matter how she tried to please him, and he never once offered to help her become the kind of woman he demanded that she be.

Year after year went by, and I don't need to tell you that they had anything but an ideal relationship. She spent most of her time worrying about whether she had upset him, and alternately feeling guilty about it, then hostile and resentful.

Now, I don't mean to give the impression that this husband was not a good man, in the truest sense of that word. He was not only good, he was perfect. But there, you see, was the very problem in their relationship. She wasn't.

Well, not being able to live with the sense of failure that was now a daily part of her thought-life, she began to wish secretly that somehow he would leave her, even if it meant he would have to die. But, alas, he was in perfect health and so very moral that divorce would be out of the question for him entirely.

As if matters weren't already bad enough, about this time she met another man. And what a man! He was everything her husband was in the way of perfection, but he had a gentleness and love about him that was definitely missing in her husband.

And then he began to woo her! And the promise of what he would be like as a husband was so tantalizing to her that in spite of her present status she could feel herself falling deeply in love with this wonderful man.

And then the day came when he put the anticipated question to her, "Will you become mine?"

Of course he knew of her present marital state, and so he came to her with a plan. Since her husband would not leave her or die, thus breaking her relationship to him, the only other solution would be for *her* to die. Then there would be a legal severance of relationship, and she would be free to marry the new husband.

Voila! What an ingenious plan.

But wait a minute!

If she were now dead, how could she be married to *anybody*, let alone this wonderful suitor?

You're way ahead of me! Right! She would have to be raised from the dead and become alive again.

AND THAT'S JUST WHAT HAPPENED TO YOU! "For since we have become united with Him in the likeness of His *death*, certainly we shall be also in the likeness of His *resurrection*. . . . Now since we have *died* with Christ, we believe that we shall also *live* with Him. . . . Even so consider yourselves to be *dead* to sin, but *alive* to God in Christ Jesus" (Romans 6:5, 8, 11).

The Characters of the Allegory

I'm sure by now you've pretty well figured out who the characters are in this allegory. You, the believer, are the wife, pictured in a before-and-after relationship with the wonderful Suitor, Jesus. The tyrannical, perfectionist husband is the Law of God. In the broader sense he also represents the sin nature and Satan himself.

These three hostile masters will never die as far as their relationship to us is concerned. So the simple solution which God arrived at was to crucify us with Jesus, thus legally breaking our relationship to these tyrants. But then, when Jesus rose from the dead—since in God's mind we were there in the grave with Him—we rose into newness of life too, and were joined into union with our beloved Suitor and Savior, Jesus.

On the basis of this legal transaction, the authority of the *old sin nature*, the *Law*, and *Satan* have been forever broken over us, Christ's bride. As far as they're concerned, we're dead to them. They can't legally touch us for a second unless we fail to realize and claim our freedom in Christ.

Just What is it That's Dead?

It's extremely important to get straight in our minds just what or who it is that's dead. I've seen people going around trying to crucify themselves and thereby trying to get rid of the power of sin and Satan. But Paul says in Romans 6:6 (paraphrased), ". . . that our old self *was* crucified with Jesus, that our body of sin [sin nature] might be rendered powerless, so that we should no longer be slaves to sin [that which the sin nature produces]."

Your "old self" is all that you were—with your appetites, drives, desires, sins, self-centeredness, and rebellion toward God—*before* you believed in Jesus and were given a "new self." At the moment you received Christ, your "old self," sometimes called the "old man," was judicially declared to be dead.

But there's nothing so great in just being dead. Being "alive" is where the action is! And that's why Jesus raised us up with Him from the dead into a whole new realm of life. This "new self" which came out of the grave could no longer be legally dominated by any of those powers which had so easily dominated the "old man."

Now, when we were raised with Christ into this new dimension of life, our "old self" was left behind in the grave. The three times it's referred to in the Bible, it's spoken of as being dead. In Romans 6:6 it specifically says that "our old self *was crucified* with Christ." In the other two passages that speak of the "old man" (Ephesians 4:22-24; Colossians 3:9, 10), the fact that he *has been* put off forever is made the basis of an appeal for a holy manner of life.

So, as far as I can see, the only enemy believers have which is really dead is their "old self" or "old man." All the other foes dedicated to the destruction of God's children are still very much alive. But the whole basis of our freedom over them is that *we* have died in our relationship to them. The authority of these adversaries —the *sin nature,* the *Law,* and *Satan*—has forever been broken in regard to the believers.

Freedom From the Power as Well as the Penalty

There are *two* aspects to the freedom which the redemptive work of Christ has made available to men.
First, we've been set free from the *penalty* of sin by
the death of Christ *for* us (1 Corinthians 15:3). That
took care of removing the barriers that separated us
from a holy and righteous God.

But secondly, His death also has provided for a daily
deliverance of believers from the *power* of sin. To
make this possible, Christ died, not only *for* sin, but to
sin (Romans 6:10). This means that He forever put
away from Himself the enemies of men's souls, and so
Paul tells us on that basis we should "consider ourselves
to be dead to sin, but alive to God in Christ Jesus"
(Romans 6:11).

A Closer Look at Our Freedom

What I'd like to do now is to consider in some depth
the extent of the freedom from the sin nature, the
principle of law, and Satan's authority which Christ's
redemption has made possible. To understand fully the
far-reaching implications of this new liberty, however,
it must be kept in mind that at the instant we believed
in Christ, the *actual* and *legal* authority of these three
great enemies of the believer was judicially severed.
But whether their control and power has, in fact, ceased
over us depends *entirely* upon whether we've claimed
our victory and depended on the indwelling Holy Spirit
to deal with their attempts at illegal access to us again.

For we must realize that these are vicious and ada-
mant enemies who are relentless in their efforts to re-
gain the dominion they had over us. As long as we're
still alive they'll be constantly at us, so we can never
relax around them and let down our guard.

But God has a provision for all of our needs, and
this case is no different. God never intended for *us* to
have to deal with the pull and lure of these tempters.
So into the "new self" which He made us to be in our

resurrection with Him, He put the third person of the Godhead, the Holy Spirit. It then became the job of this indwelling Holy Spirit to deal with the temptations of the old sin nature, the Law, and Satan. We'll look at the work of the Holy Spirit in greater detail in the next chapter.

In chapter four I discussed in depth what the sin nature is and how it operates in man, so I only want to briefly review that here, and then look at the extent of our freedom from it.

The Old Sin Nature

The old sin nature is that predisposition toward rebellion against God with which we're all born. It's the old sinful Adamic nature that we inherited from Adam. That's what Paul meant in Romans 5:12: "Through one man [*Adam*] sin [*the sin nature and its product, sin*] entered into the world."

This nature is sometimes referred to as "sin" in the singular. That's the way Paul uses it in the principle passages of Scripture which teach about this sinful nature. Romans 6, 7, and 8. It's also spoken of as "the flesh" in some passages, although "the flesh" is not always meant to refer to that "fallenness" in us which is generally connoted by the use of the word "flesh." It occasionally has a neutral or even holy meaning, but that's almost always evident by the immediate context.

In chapter four I told about the science-fiction movie where men from outer space planted tiny receiving sets in the back of the heads of their victims here on earth. Then when they went back into space, they transmitted instructions to their robot-like victims, who were programmed to obey.

That's much the way the old sin nature works in us. It's the "enemy agent" inside us that's constantly being energized by tactics of Satan to keep us from living holy and victorious lives. It's not a hopeless situation, though, and in this and the next chapter we'll see clearly what God has done to set us free from our spiritual enemies.

Satan Gets at Us Through the Law

One of the favorite tactics of Satan in trying to keep believers enslaved is to get them on the treadmill of trying to live for God by keeping all His laws. In chapter eleven of my book, *Satan Is Alive and Well on Planet Earth*,[1] I show what the Law is, how it works on man, and why it's completely impotent as an instrument for helping us live holy lives. I'm going to re-emphasize some of that material here and show that the Law has no more legal jurisdiction over us. We've been set free from it.

First of all, I need to deal with the subject of what makes us sin in our daily lives as believers. Sometimes when we sin we like to say, "The Devil made me do it," and there's usually a twinkle in our eye when we say it. It may help us get off the hook in our own minds, but we can't blame Satan for all our sinning.

There are two ingredients necessary for a person to sin. In Romans 7:5 Paul says, "For while we were in the flesh [before we became believers], the *sinful passions,* which were *aroused by the Law,* were at work in the members of our body to bear fruit for death."

Here Paul indicates there are two things at work within a nonbeliever to make him sin: his sinful passions, or sin nature as it's sometimes called, and the Law. When the Law stirs up the sinful passion, rebellion against the Law occurs and that's what the Bible calls "sin."

This principle of law works exactly the same way in us after we've become a child of God, for Paul says, "I would not have come to know sin except through the Law; for I would not have known about coveting if the Law had not said, 'You shall not covet.' But sin, taking opportunity through the commandment, produced in me coveting of every kind; for apart from the Law sin is dead" (Romans 7:7, 8).

Psychology has noticed this same tendency in man to do just the opposite of what he's commanded to do.

---

[1] *Satan Is Alive and Well on Planet Earth* (Grand Rapids: Zondervan Publishing House, 1972).

We call it the "law of reverse psychology." If you want someone to do something, tell him to do just the opposite. Most parents have figured this out before their children get very old.

The Law is Not the Culprit

I know that all this tends to put the law in a bad light, whether God's law or man's law. But the law isn't the real problem. Those sinful passions or sin natures that get stirred up by the Law are the problem.

Now, you might be wondering why God gave the Law if He knew it would work against us rather than for us. Well, first of all, God knew that ultimately the Law *would* work for us when it had brought us to the place God intended for it to. We'll look at that in a minute, but first let's see why God gave the Law.

The first reason is to show man what sin is. Law is a principle which guides our behavior by setting up standards of conduct and threatening certain consequences if the standards aren't met.

There are several kinds of law set forth in the Bible. There's the "law of conscience" referred to in Romans 2:14, 15: "For when Gentiles who do not have the Law [of Moses] do instinctively the things of the Law, these, not having the Law, are a law to themselves, in that they show the work of the Law written in their hearts, their conscience bearing witness, and their thoughts alternately accusing or else defending themselves."

This law of conscience means that even people who've never heard of the Law of Moses, which is God's law, still have an innate law of good and evil and are responsible to live in the light of that.

God rejected the law of conscience as a means for man to know Him because the conscience was too easily seared. About the time that Moses came along, the people had so little consciousness of what sin was that God saw their need for an objective standard or law that would forever nail down what He considered to be sin.

This law was what we've referred to as "the Law of Moses." This was not only the Ten Commandments, but also hundreds of other laws which regulated how people were to live their daily lives.

Then when Jesus came and preached the Sermon on the Mount and gave all His other admonitions during His teaching, and later the Apostle amplified these and added more rules and regulations, this was still another kind of law called "the law of the New Testament."

All these kinds of law were given for the purpose of defining and showing man what sin was. That's the first reason for God giving the Law.

The second reason these laws were given was to provoke man's sin nature to sin more. Paul said in Romans 5:20, "And the Law came in that the transgression might increase." God wants the unbeliever to get so loaded with sin that there's no way he can fail to see how utterly sinful he is and how much he needs a Savior.

Paul's pitiful story of his tangle with the Law in Romans 7 shows that the Law provokes even the believer to sin more. He said in verses 7-9 that the Law told him he shouldn't covet, but his sin nature, aroused by that law, produced all the more coveting. He said he was once a fruitful, alive believer, with his tendency to covet, well under control. Then all of a sudden he got to dwelling on the fact that the Law said not to covet and then this commandment, activating the sin nature into rebelling, caused him to die. He didn't mean to die physically or to die spiritually. The word "die" here means to cease walking in dependence upon the Holy Spirit and so *fellowship* with God dies, not relationship.

The third reason God gave the law was to drive us to despair of self-effort. It seems God is working against Himself to get us to sin more, but this is His way of bringing us to total despair of self-effort in seeking to live for Him. You see, the harder we try to live for God by trying to keep His laws, the more we fail and that's what He intended. And the more we fail, the more we have to admit our helplessness and human inadequacy. When we finally get to that place of despair, we're ready for the fourth reason God gave the Law.

The fourth reason God gave the Law was to bring the unbeliever to Christ for salvation and the believer to the Holy Spirit for His empowering. Paul uses a good illustration of this fact in Galatians 3:24,25, where he says, "The Law has become our tutor to lead us to Christ, that we may be justified by faith. But now that faith has come, we are no longer under a tutor."

A tutor was a specially chosen slave whose job it was to take a Roman child by the hand every morning and lead him to the school. He would wait there until the lessons were done and then lead the child home again. Once the child's school days were over, he no longer needed his "tutor."

That's exactly what the Law does, and it was the ultimate purpose of God's giving the Law. The Law takes the unbeliever by the hand and leads him to Christ for salvation. But the Law also takes the believer by the hand and leads him to the Holy Spirit who is the only source of power to be and do what the Law demands.

The Law Has Done its Job

The job of the Law was to show us what sin was and actually make us sin more. Then it was meant to drive us to despair of our self-efforts in trying to live for God and ultimately to bring us to Christ for salvation and for the moment-by-moment power to live a godly and victorious life. When this progression is finished, then the Law is finally done with the believer. Its purpose is finished and we have no more need for it, because it's been replaced by the giving of the Holy Spirit to dwell in us and actually produce the results of the law in and through us.

But, even though the law is through with us, we won't

let go of it. In place of the Law of God, we've sub-
stituted man-made rules and taboos for how to live the
Christian life. Instead of teaching people how to walk
in the Spirit, it's been easier to pass a few rules pro-
hibiting this behavior and that. All this has served to
do is stimulate the sin natures of the believers. It has
never produced holy living and it never will.

Anarchy is Not Freedom

However, it would be folly to go around telling believers that they're no longer responsible to keep God's
law unless you also told them about the grounds of
their deliverance from it. Those grounds are twofold.

First, if you'll recall the allegory I started this chapter with, you'll remember that the husband in that story
was the Law. When the woman could no longer bear
the condemnation she lived under for her failure to
perform to his satisfaction, she allowed herself to be
put to death and then raised into a whole new life,
legally free and severed from her old husband's
authority.

Now, that's just what's happened to each of us in our
relationship to the Law. It will never die, but that
shouldn't bother us in the least since we've died to it.
Knowing this as a fact is paramount in actually experiencing freedom from the Law. If you don't "reckon"
on this deadness, as Paul says in Romans 6, then you'll
find yourself being intimidated by law of every kind.
Someone will tell a story of how he witnessed to five
waitresses and they all received Christ, and before
long you'll feel so guilty about going into a restaurant
without witnessing to the waitresses that you'll probably
never eat out again.

I often hear people accuse others of putting them
under the Law, and it's true that some people do
wrongly emphasize that as a means of living a Christian
life. But if you allow yourself to be put under Law,
that's your own fault because God has provided your
freedom from it and it's up to you to reckon on that
deliverance.

The Spirit Replaced the Law

I said there are two reasons why we can tell believers they are no longer responsible to live under the law. I've just explained the first, and the second is, "If you are led by the Spirit, you are not under the Law" (Galatians 5:18). The Spirit is our replacement for the Law. He wrote it, and He's perfectly able to keep it in us as we walk by faith, trusting Him to do so.

In this same context Paul says, "Walk by the Spirit, and you will not carry out the desire of the flesh [sin nature]" (Galatians 5:16).

So you can see that freedom from the Law and the sin nature doesn't mean you have no one over you in authority at all. That's anarchy and it's anything but freedom. Real freedom comes when we submit ourselves to the moment-by-moment control of the indwelling Holy Spirit and allow Him to empower us to live for God.

Freedom From Satan's Domination

So far we've looked at two enemies from which we've been set free by Christ's redemptive work on the cross, our sin natures and the principle of living by law instead of grace. Now we'll look at the third area in which we've been given our freedom: the area of Satan's dominion and authority.

One of the great effects of the death of Christ, and your death with Him, is that in it you were set free from Satan's and demons' authority and control. They can no longer use that illegal lie on you, "You must give in to this temptation, because I'm still the master of your life."

The key passage which amplifies this truth is Acts 26:18, in which God has said He has opened people's eyes, "so that they may turn from darkness to light and from the dominion of Satan to God." The word "dominion" here means "authority"; Satan doesn't hold any authority or legal right to tell you what to do anymore. Your sin debt was paid by Jesus at the cross, and when He rose from the dead, "He made you alive together with Him, having forgiven us all our transgressions" (Colossians 2:13).

The resurrection of Christ proved to be Satan's final undoing. Paul tells us that when Jesus rose from the dead, He disarmed the rulers and authorities—referring to Satan and demons—and made a public spectacle of them in showing His triumph over them. He's now the head over all these rulers and authorities (see Colossians 2:15,10).

But there's a critical truth here that's generally not understood by believers. Since we were crucified with Christ and rose with Him, His victory over Satan and demons is our victory too. Their legal right to touch us is forever gone.

A clear illustration of this truth is the story that follows. It's a case on record from many years back.

The Case of the "Deposed Captain"

A ship at sea had a captain so ruthless and brutal to his men that they became desperate and fearful for their individual safety.

In maritime law, the captain of a ship is the absolute master until officially relieved from command by the country with which the ship is registered.

The first mate aboard the vessel was an understanding and humanly sympathetic man, respected by all hands. After much personal consideration and real insistence on the part of the entire crew, he radioed the home port, reporting the atrocities of the captain against his men, and requested permission to assume command at once.

A message was flashed back commissioning him to take official command. The former captain was to be relieved of all authority effective immediately and would be brought home aboard the ship to stand trial.

He was allowed freedom to move about on deck, but it was made clear to the entire crew that he had been relieved of his position of authority.

Not long after that, the former captain decided to test his power. A seaman was busy at work, happily enjoying the leadership of the new commander. The old captain came by, jerked the man aside, and began issuing stern orders. The seaman had been so accustomed to following his commands that he instinctively buckled under. And as soon as he started to obey, the old captain proceeded to lay it on all the more.

Amidst the verbal barrage, the seaman came to his senses and realized the man no longer had authority over him to bark out these insulting commands. He began to resist—and got the beating of his life. Bruised and battered, he told his rightful commander of the incident.

He left, reminded by the new captain that the next time a confrontation developed, the former commander held absolutely no authority over him or any of the crew. There was no reason even to listen to the old man. And should another incident arise, the men were to subdue him, on the direct orders of the new ship's captain, and he would be held in the brig.

Set Free to Serve

Let's face it. We're at war. But God wants us to know that we no longer have to give in to the demands of our sin natures, that we're no longer under the law, and that we've been liberated from the authority and dominion of Satan. The ransom was paid by Jesus, and we've been set free from the slave market of sin. The only slavery for us now is our willing slavery to Jesus out of love and gratitude.

A wonderful story illustrates this.

In the days of slavery in ancient Rome, a notorious and cruel slaveholder was in the Roman slave market to purchase some additional slaves. That particular day there was a stranger there also, a kindly man who was new at the market. He bought slaves in order to set them free.

A slave was put up on the dock, and the bidding started. The cruel man opened the bid, and the good man immediately set forth a competitive bid. The prices offered began to soar to dizzy heights as the men bid back and forth.

Finally the good man named a price so high that the wicked slaveholder couldn't match it.

As the new owner walked up to the proprietor of the slave market to make payment of the ransom, the slave marched over behind his new master and prepared to follow him.

The good man who had bought the slave turned around and said, "You're free to go. I bought you to set you free." And he started to walk away.

"Wait a minute," the slave answered. "If I'm a free man, then I'm free to follow you. My desire is to serve you out of gratitude for what you've done for me."

What this slave experienced is just what Christ has done for us. He's set us free from the impossible demands of the Law. He's taken us out of Satan's slave market by stripping him of his authority over us. And He's delivered us from the tyranny of our sin natures by giving us a new nature and the indwelling Holy Spirit to empower it.

But not only has Jesus Christ set our *spirits* free through His redemption, He's also provided for the ultimate redemption of our *bodies* (Romans 8:23). Inasmuch as He's already paid the ransom price for our physical redemption, this refers to the resurrection of our physical bodies that's yet to come—and in the near future, I believe.

When a believer dies, his soul and spirit go immediately to be with the Lord in heaven, but his body goes into the grave and back to dust (2 Corinthians 5:8). But the day is coming when all God's children who are in the graves will hear His trumpet and shout and come out of the graves with the same bodies they went in with—only now they'll be made whole and immortal. Then those believers who are alive will be instantly changed into immortal bodies and they'll go to be with Jesus also, without having to go through physical death.[1]

This physical redemption—as well as our freedom from Satan, the Law, and sin—is what Paul refers to as God's "mercies" toward us who believe. On the basis of these, he urges us who are believers to "present your bodies a living and holy sacrifice, acceptable to God, which is your spiritual service of worship" (Romans 12:1).

God doesn't demand that we become His servants, but Paul says it's the only reasonable thing to do in light of all God's done for us.

---

[1] For a fuller treatment of this subject of the ultimate redemption of believers' bodies, see chapter 4 of the author's book, *There's a New World Coming* (Vision House Publishers: Santa Ana, California, 1973).

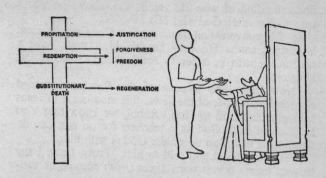

Chapter Seventeen

Regeneration

Every spring the whole earth gives testimony to the truth of regeneration as it emerges from its wintry slumber and comes forth with fresh, green vegetation from the soil. Plant life is thus reborn or given new life. What has been dead for a time now comes back to life.

But as great a phenomenon as it is to put a kernel of corn into the ground and then watch new life spring forth from the dead kernel, the greater miracle of regeneration of the human spirit has been made possible because of Christ's substitutionary death on the cross. The moment we place our trust in that death in our behalf, the Holy Spirit of God impregnates our dead human spirits with the eternal life of God and we're reborn spiritually.

One of the clearest declarations of man's need to be born again, or "from above," is a conversation Jesus had with the leading religious teacher of Israel, Nicodemus. This was a sincere and humanly righteous man, and the fact that he sought Jesus out to try to get an

understanding of who He really was, shows he was a
true seeker after God and His kingdom.

In this conversation Jesus revealed one of the most
important truths He ever taught. Man must have a
spiritual rebirth in order to comprehend God and His
kingdom.

"Now there was a man of the Pharisees, named
Nicodemus, a ruler of the Jews; this man came to Jesus
by night, and said to Him, 'Rabbi, we know that You
have come from God as a teacher; for no one can do
these signs that You do unless God is with him.'

"Jesus answered and said to him, 'Truly, truly, I say
to you, unless one is born again [*from above*], he cannot see the kingdom of God.'

"Nicodemus said to Him, 'How can a man be born
when he is old? He cannot enter a second time into his
mother's womb and be born, can he?'

"Jesus answered, 'Truly, truly, I say to you, unless
one is born of water and the Spirit, he cannot enter
into the kingdom of God. That which is born of the
flesh is flesh; and that which is born of the Spirit is
spirit.

" 'Do not marvel that I said to you, "You must be
born again."

" 'The wind blows where it wishes and you hear the
sound of it, but do not know where it comes from and
where it is going; so is every one who is born of the
Spirit' " (John 3:1-8). Or, "You can see the effect on
their lives, even though you can't see what caused it."

The Re-Education of Nicodemus

Nicodemus's response to what Jesus said was simple
and straightforward: "How can these things be?"

Jesus answered and said to him, "Are you *the*
teacher of Israel, and do not understand these things"
(John 3:9,10)? "You mean to say, Nicodemus, that
you're the leading religious teacher of Israel and you've
never realized that there was a spiritual dimension of
man that was missing?"

You see, Nicodemus prided himself on the fact that

he was born into the race of God's chosen people. He was banking his eventual salvation too heavily on his physical heritage. That's why Jesus went right to the real issue and pulled the rug out from under him. In essence, what he told Nicodemus was that "he wasn't all there."

Mankind "Isn't All There!"

I'm sure you've already noticed that something's desperately wrong with people in this world. A casual glance at the morning news is enough to put you under a gloom cloud all day. Nothing but murders, scandal, war, crooked politicians, divorces, and so forth.

The thing that's wrong with people is, they aren't all there. The most important dimension of their being is nonfunctioning, their human spirit. Without it, nothing else seems to go right for very long in a life.

In chapter six on Spiritual Death, we saw a diagram of the three parts of man—spirit, soul, and body. We briefly looked at what these were, but now in this chapter I want to show how they work in a believer. It's absolutely imperative to have a clear understanding of the functions of these three parts of our being, or we can't put our finger on the source of the problem when things go haywire and don't work right.

The Creation of Man's Two Kinds of Life

When God decided to make man, He picked up a handful of dust and shaped it into a man. Then He breathed into this creation's nose the breath of lives, and man became a living soul (Genesis 2:7).

Two kinds of life were born that day, *soulish life (psuche)* which started the heart beating and blood flowing and created the soul and personality of man. And *spiritual life (zoe)* which became the human spirit in man and enabled him to communicate with God who is spirit. These two kinds of life found their home in the physical body of man, and there was harmony in their interworkings.

The Bible says man became a "living soul" (KJV). The soul was to stand in the center, between the spirit and body, and be the merging place of these two. It was to be the part of man through which the spirit and body expressed themselves. It stood between these two worlds, yet it belonged integrally to both. Since the soul has free will, it was to decide which would dominate the life, the spirit or the body.

Before Adam sinned, the spirit dominated his soul and body, but with the free will he was given as part of his soul, Adam made the decision to disobey God; and when he did, the spirit of man underwent a violent change. Its capacity to communicate with God ceased, and a deadness developed in man's relationship with God. The tragic result of this was that the soul and body of men were now left without a spiritual monitor and their whole development *excluded* the enlightening and restraining power of God. Instead of being "God" centered, man became "self" centered. Instead of being a "flower" out of the Creator's hand, he became a "weed" growing wild, with no cultivation or grooming.

Let's look at each one of these functions of man separately now, using the diagram on the next page to help visualize these critical truths.

The Spirit

The obvious first step in spiritual growth is regeneration. This is where the human spirit of man plays its most important role. When Adam and Eve were created, they were given a human spirit that enabled them to commune with God. Their spirit did *not* contain the uncreated eternal life of God, however. As long as they were in the garden they had God Himself there, and that was all they needed for then.

Right in the middle of the garden, where it couldn't be overlooked, was the Tree of Life. This was available for man to eat of anytime he wanted to, and I believe this would have given him the eternal life of God if he had eaten of it.

But there was another tree there also, the Tree of

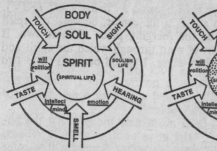

MAN, BEFORE THE FALL   MAN, AFTER THE FALL

Knowledge of Good and Evil. We've already seen in past chapters that this tree was the "test" tree. Man was forbidden to eat of it. To do so meant he was vaunting his will over God's, and the consequence of that was going to be a loss of spiritual life and communion with God (Genesis 2:17).

As soon as he had eaten, however, God said, " 'Behold, the man has become like one of Us, knowing good and evil; and now, lest he stretch out his hand, and take also from the Tree of Life, and eat, and live forever,' he must be sent out of the Garden and his way back to the Tree of Life prohibited (Genesis 3:22-24). God couldn't let spiritually dead men be given eternal life without all the necessary renovations inside them that would fit them for eternity with God. And those renovations were going to be the most costly thing God ever undertook. They wouldn't come cheaply.

The Renovation of the Spirit

The renovation of your spirit begins the day you believe in Jesus' substitutionary death for you and thank Him for dying in your place. Some people like to use the concept of inviting Jesus to come into their heart. That's based on Jesus' statement in Revelation 3:20, "Behold, I stand at the door and knock; if any one hears My voice and opens the door, I will come in to him, and will dine [fellowship] with him, and he with Me." The *door* referred to in this verse is likened to the door of their will.

But whatever your mental picture is at the moment you receive Christ as your personal Savior, the important thing is that your nonfunctioning, dormant human spirit is finally revived and given a new source of spiritual life, the Holy Spirit.

Sometimes it's been mistakenly thought that the human spirit doesn't exist in us until we've been reborn, but there are too many verses of Scripture that refer to the spirit in unregenerate men for us to be dogmatic about this. I believe the spirit has continued to exist in men right from the day Adam sinned, but what we inherit from him is a spirit void of its ability to communicate with God or be the recipient of God's communication to us. So in every real sense it's dead, because it isn't working the way it was intended. The great French philosopher and theologian, Pascal, called this spiritual void in man a "God-shaped vacuum which only Christ could fill."

Actually it's much like a lamp to which the electricity is turned off. The lamp is good for nothing but ornamentation until it's connected to its source of power and life. But it doesn't cease being a lamp just because it isn't functioning the way it should.

The Dead Spirit Does Serve a Function

Even though the human spirit is void of any spiritual life in the one who's not been born again, still its very inactive presence in the unbeliever plays an important role. It serves as a constant reminder that something very basic is missing from our inner beings. It's as Augustine said, "You have made us for yourself, O God, and our hearts are restless until they find their rest in You."

Until the One who made us comes to dwell in His rightful place in our spirits, we'll never feel complete. There'll always be a sense of something missing. This accounts for the many things that people give themselves to hedonistically in an effort to find inner fulfillment and peace. An overemphasis in the use of sex, money, fame, power, beauty, pleasure, religion, and good deeds is often symptomatic of an effort to fill the inner void in the spirit which only Christ can fill.

The Light in Men Comes Back On

The Bible pictures the unregenerate man as "walking in darkness." That's why he can't see that all the things he tries to substitute for Jesus in his life are only delusive counterfeits. When Adam sinned, his spirit became darkened without God's inner illumination. His spiritual light went out.

But at the heart of God's plan to regenerate men was His intention of restoring the light to the darkened spirits of men. Listen to how the Apostle John pictured Jesus as the One who would bring the light back to men. "In Him [Jesus] was life; and the life was the *light* of men . . . [He] was the true light which, coming into the world, enlightens every man" (John 1:4,9).

Peter said the same thing of Jesus when he wrote of Him as the One who has "called you out of darkness into His marvelous light" (1 Peter 2:9b).

But the greatest authority on the subject of "light" was Jesus Himself. He called Himself "the Light of the World." "He who follows Me shall not walk in the darkness," He said, "but shall have the light of life" (John 8:12).

So when a person is born again, the light really goes on inside him. For the first time he's able to understand the things of God and the spiritual realm. He prays and knows for certain that he's getting through because he now has God's life and light in him. And God begins to shine that new light onto his path and show him what His will for his life is.

Walk as "Children of Light"

It's because we've been given this inner light that Paul admonishes us in the way he does in Ephesians 5:1-8.

There he talks about a number of sins that unregenerate men freely participate in: greed, immorality,
silly and dirty talk, coveting, and so forth. Then he
says, "Do not be partakers with them, for you were
formerly darkness, but now you are light in the Lord;
walk as children of light." (verses 7, 8).

I think that's a terrific description of born-again believers—"Children of Light." If there's anything this
dark old world needs, it's light. You can see that by
the fantastic rise in popularity of psychics, astrologers,
prophets, and others trying to find out what's going on.
But the only true source of light as to where the world's
going, and how to be prepared to live at peace in the
world, are the "Children of Light." That's why Jesus
said, "Let your light shine before men in such a way
that they may see your good works, and glorify your
Father who is in heaven" (Matthew 5:16).

Let's take a look now at the main function of the
regenerated spirit.

The Sixth Sense: Faith

When a man is born again, life is restored to his spirit
and there, in the "inner man," he's able to understand,
love, and worship God in the deep way in which the
new nature longs to. And the things of the spiritual
realm are no longer unreal and alien. The Holy Spirit
comes to take up residence in his recreated spirit and
begins to reveal the mind and heart of God to him.

This restoration of spiritual life gives back to man
what Adam lost. It's called the "sixth sense," *faith.*
Faith is the eyesight of the spirit. It causes us to reach
out to God to know Him. Faith enables us to believe
that when God says He'll do something for us, He will!
The body has its five senses that make the material
world real, and the knowledge man gains through them
is called the "human viewpoint" of life (HVP for
short). But the intimate knowledge of God can only
be known through the sixth sense, faith, and it's called
the "divine viewpoint" of life (DVP for short).

Only the person who's been born again has a sixth

sense and thus both these viewpoints in him. The unregenerate person has only the human viewpoint.

These two viewpoints of life are very often in conflict with each other. The five senses continually pour into the mind the world's view on everything, and this is a viewpoint that says man determines his own destiny and God is not a relevant force. It says, "If you wanna' make it, kid, *you've* got what it takes. Get in there and pitch!"

On the other hand, the sixth sense says, "Look, God made you. He put you together atom by atom and then after you'd turned your back on Him, He provided a redemption for you. Now don't you think you can trust a God like that to be able to handle whatever this problem is you're trying to cope with on your own?"

And so, both the recreated human spirit (*the sixth sense*) and the flesh (*the five senses*) bombard the soul (*mind*) with their viewpoints, and these two are almost always opposed to one another.

For example, Paul promises the believers that "God causes all things to work together for good to those who love God" (Romans 8:28). Now, suppose when you walked into work this morning, your boss met you and said you were fired. Through the senses of sight and hearing, this (*humanly speaking*) very bad information came into your mind. At the same time, through your sixth sense, faith, God reminded you of His promise that this will all work together for your good.

At this point *you* must decide which viewpoint of life is going to dominate you. If the HVP dominates, you'll probably panic and grab air! But if you choose to deliberately shut out the five senses and only listen to the sixth sense, you'll experience the calm and peace of God, because you'll be assured that the problem is in His able hands.

Faith Depends on God's Faithfulness

Now, this is really all that faith is. It's our response to God's ability to handle our lives. If I really believe He's able, then I'll automatically have faith. If I don't know how trustworthy He is, then no amount of spiritual gimmicks is going to make me trust Him at a time when I need faith.

Faith is such a misunderstood concept. I often hear people praying for more faith, but strictly speaking, that's a wrong prayer. Once you've been born again and had your sixth sense restored to your spirit, you now have all the faith you can ever get.

You see, faith operates in your re-created spirit just as the five senses operate in your body. Take the sense of sight, for example. You can have 20/20 vision and yet look at a mountain fifty miles away and not see it very clearly. In that case you don't need better eyesight; you need to get closer to the mountain so that it will come into better focus.

That's the way faith works. We're all given 20/20 faith when we're born again. But faith needs an object in order for it to function, and Jesus is that object, revealed to us through His Word.

If Jesus has not seemed as real to you as you might want, and you've felt that you needed more faith to bring Him closer, I hope you can see from this that what you really need is to get a closer view of this wonderful Object. You do this by getting into His Word and starting to see just who He is and what He's done for you and promises still to give you. Your faith won't grow, but your concept of Jesus will, and the end result will be the same in your life. You'll start to believe Him more, and you'll find yourself loving and responding to Him in a way you've never done before.

The Soul

Whereas the spirit is that part of man which makes him conscious of God and relates him to Him, the soul is that part of us which relates us to ourselves and gives us self-consciousness. Then through the various functions of the soul—namely *mind, emotion,* and *will*—we're able to give expression to our inner selves.

The soul allows us to reveal our personalities. It

draws upon both the conscious and subconscious minds which are part of it. It's the part of man where the spirit and body find their external expression.

In the Bible people are occasionally referred to as "souls." This is because God views the soul as the man himself. A man without a soul is a dead man because the soul is the actual life in us. The Hebrew word for soul, *nephesh,* is often translated "life" in the Old Testament. The New Testament uses the Greek word *psuche* for both "soul" and "soul life" and it's often translated as "life."

"The *life* [soul] of the flesh is in the blood" (Leviticus 17:11).

"I do not consider my life [soul] of any account . . ." (Acts 20:24).

"The good shepherd lays down His life [soul] for the sheep" (John 10:11).

Adam "Blew It," But He Was No Dummy!

When we're born into this world, the only kind of life we have is soulish life *(psuche).* That's what we educate, train, discipline, pamper, and eagerly protect. The power in a human soul is not unlimited, but it's certainly very great.

When you stop to think about the fantastic degree of intelligence Adam had in his soul, it makes you believe a little bit more in the *downward* spiral of men's minds, not the upward climb.

Adam was given the dominion over the whole earth and everything in it (Genesis 1:27,28). It took tremendous organizational skill and know-how to accomplish just that task. But that wasn't all he had to do; he was given the job of naming all the animals. You and I could take a dictionary and write out the names of all the hundreds of animals and birds, but trying to memorize them would be another job. Yet Adam thought up those names.

Adam was also a skilled gardener because he was given the job of keeping the Garden of Eden in shape. I know what a job it is just to try to keep my own small garden fertilized, pruned, and groomed. But the size of the Garden of Eden must have been staggering. Yet, evidently it was no problem for Adam. because he never even knew what it was to sweat until he was driven from the Garden and his soul began to deteriorate in its great power (see Genesis 3:19).

Man's Self-Centeredness Begins

From the pattern of what Adam's soul was capable of, we can see what God had in mind for man originally in his soulish life. Unfortunately, when Adam sinned, the soul was no longer under the control of the spirit, and so all it could do was become more and more *self*-conscious and *self*-centered. Men began to think only about themselves, of meeting their own needs and having their own fleshly desires fulfilled. The soul—which had been intended by God to be the place of the balanced expression of the complete man, *body, soul,* and *spirit*—now became the center of the fallen "ego" or "self." The spirit of man was dead as far as its influence over the soul was concerned.

The Apostle Paul coined a name for man in this condition. He called him, "the soulish man" (1 Corinthians 2:14). That's because the soul, with its mind, emotions, will, and capitulation to the desires of the flesh, was what dominated the man. In this same verse of Scripture Paul speaks of the limitations of the soulish man; "But a natural man [soulish man] does not accept the things of the Spirit of God; for they are foolishness to him, and he cannot understand them, because they are spiritually appraised." The point is, if a man were spiritually dead, he could train his mind to the level of Ph.D. but still have no spiritual discernment.

Body (Flesh)

So far we've seen briefly the makeup of the spirit and soul in man. But before we can look at how God has transformed them by the new birth, we've got to get a look at the body, or flesh, of men and see its role in the whole man.

The body is the part of us that's world-conscious. It's the house of the soul and spirit. But it's intimately united with the soul because the life of the soul (*psuche*) is what keeps the physical body alive. After the fall of man, the soul and body tended to merge into one, with one or the other being dominant. If it was the soul, then the person was artistic or intellectual. If the body dominated, then the person was more sensuous or athletic.

The five senses located in the physical body are the mechanisms which bring the reality of the material world into the consciousness of the person. They're like windows of the soul. In order for the senses to operate, however, they must have an external stimulus of some kind. For example, there has to be an object in order for sight to function. Likewise, there has to be a sound in order for hearing to occur, and so forth.

One of the basic principles that many psychologists teach is that man is a product of his environment. What that means is simply that we're the sum total of all the things that have touched our lives. All these experiences and forces that have molded our lives have come into us through the agency of the five senses. Of course, the way we've handled this information once it's come into our minds is influenced greatly by our inherited temperaments and traits. And once we become believers, the indwelling Holy Spirit influences our reactions to the things that happen to us.

The Flesh is No Friend of God

The actual substance of the flesh is not what's usually meant by the references to it in the Bible. It generally refers to a principle of rebellion against God that's permeated all that we are in the Old Man. It's so unreformable that God didn't even try to salvage it in the new creation. He simply pronounced it hopelessly re-

bellious and then proceeded to lay down the principles
for how we could live in victory over it.

Whatever is wrapped up in the concept of the flesh,
all men have it. But it's the *only* realm that unregenerate men can operate in, since soulish life is the
only kind of life they have. The born-again person still
has the flesh, but he doesn't have to live and operate in
that realm because he's also alive in the realm of the
spirit by virtue of his spiritual rebirth.

Listen to how the Apostle Paul viewed the matter of
the flesh as he wrote to the believers at Ephesus. "And
you were dead in your trespasses and sins, in which
you formerly walked according to the course of this
world, according to the prince of the power of the air,
of the spirit that is now working in the sons of disobedience.

"Among them we too all formerly lived in the *lusts
of our flesh*, indulging the *desires of the flesh* and of the
mind, and were by nature children of wrath, even as
the rest" (Ephesians 2:1-3).

As much as some people might not like to think
about it, God has a very dim view of the flesh whether
it's in a believer or an unbeliever. That's because the
flesh has a very dim view of God. In fact, Paul says, it's
hostile to God and anyone who operates consistently
in the realm of the flesh can't please God (Romans
8:7, 8). He even says that the mind that's habitually
controlled by the flesh is evidence that the person is
still spiritually dead (Romans 8:6). In Romans 7:18
in which Paul is speaking about the problem which he,
as a believer, still had with the flesh, he said, "For I
know that nothing good dwells in me, that is, in my
flesh."

It's obvious from these verses and many more that
there is a "fallenness" about us that's inherent in the
flesh. This rebellious streak is sometimes spoken of as
"sin," as in 1 John 1:8: "If we say that we have no sin,
we are deceiving ourselves and the truth is not in us."
The flesh is also synonymous with the Old Sin Nature
which as we've already seen is that force in us which is

dedicated to resisting God in our lives. All men are born with this curse, and it's *not* removed from us when we're born again, although victory over it is made available to us.

The Two Sides of the Flesh

At the Fall, the body and soul merged together to comprise this spiritual foe we know as the flesh. It includes the "*attitudes* of the flesh" as well as the "*works* of the flesh." These two sides of the flesh will continue to manifest themselves through the life of the believer to the degree that he allows his soul to dominate him, rather than his spirit.

The "attitudes of the flesh" are all the ideas, plans, schemes, imaginations, and good works which proceed out of the human mind without the Holy Spirit being the source of them. They can be either good or bad, as the world views such things, but in God's estimation they're all unacceptable because the flesh is the source of them, not the spirit. These "attitudes of the flesh" are sometimes hard to detect because they deal in the realm of ideas and thoughts and often seem so noble. However, these soulish activities *always* have self somewhere at the center.

Self-confidence and *self*-reliance are two notable traits of the soul. The world applauds these and they seem like such admirable qualities, but God says they indicate a reliance on the flesh rather than on the indwelling Holy Spirit.

The "works of the flesh" are often referred to as the "lusts of the flesh," and these refer to the sins which are stimulated by the fleshy drives and passions. These are fairly easy to spot in a life because they're usually pretty gross and overt. Paul lists some of them in Galatians 5:19-31: "Now the *deeds of the flesh* are evident, which are: immorality, impurity, sensuality, idolatry, sorcery, enmities, strife, jealousy, outbursts of anger, disputes, dissensions, factions, envyings, drunkenness, carousings, and things like these."

The Flesh is Tricky

Where believers get tripped up is in not realizing that
the flesh is not only the *sin* tendency, but also the *self*
tendency. It's easier to spot the overt sins that originate
out of the desires and demands of the flesh. But the
"attitude" sins of the flesh are much more subtle and
more acceptable in the Christian community. That's
because, like Lady Clairol, "only the Lord knows for
sure" what the source of the attitude is.

For instance, as a kid growing up I used to be
preached at all the time, by preachers and Sunday
school teachers, that drinking, smoking, and going to
movies were sinful. But I never heard any sermons
about the evils of teaching a Sunday school class if
you weren't filled with the Spirit, or of preaching a
message when the preacher and his wife had problems
between them which they needed to reconcile.

You see, these are works of the flesh of which only
God and you know whether He's the source. But if He
isn't, then these good deeds are every bit as unacceptable in His sight as those overt sins of the flesh.

The Renovation of Regeneration

One of my favorite songs has the first line, "I believe in
miracles, I've seen a soul set free."

To me, in this age of miracles, the greatest one of all
is the marvel of God undoing the internal damage to
man's spirit, soul, and body and bringing the harmony
and balance He originally designed us for.

Paul amplifies this when he says in 2 Corinthians
5:17, "Therefore if any man is in Christ, he is a new
creature; the old things passed away; behold, new
things have come."

What were those old things that passed away?

Basically, your "Old Man" passed away. (*May he
rest in peace!*) That's everything you were in Adam:
spiritually dead, hostile to God, under the Law, headed
for eternity in hell, obliged to serve Satan, dominated
by your soulish life and the flesh, not indwelt by the

Holy Spirit, unrighteous, condemned, and self-centered.

The Apostle Paul named this fact of the "Old Man" having been crucified as the basis for all those things we were in Adam losing their power over us. "Knowing this, that our old man *was crucified* with Christ, that our body of sin *might be made powerless,* that we should no longer be slaves to sin; for he who has died is acquitted of sin" (Romans 6:6, 7 paraphrased).

But as I said in the last chapter, there's no particular power in simply being dead. We went into the grave as the "Old Man," but we came out in our resurrection with Christ as a "New Man." Paul stresses that in Colossians 3:2-10. Here he tells the believers to set their minds on things above, not on the things of earth, for they *have* died to those things and are simply to consider it as a fact. Then he urges them to put aside things like anger, wrath, ill-will, dirty language, and lies, because they *have* laid aside the Old Man (*self*) with its evil practices and *have* already put on the New Man (*self*) who is in the process of being renovated into the image of God.

Off With the Old Man — On With the New

Not only did old things pass away when you were born again, but all things became new in your relationship with God and inside of you. Everything that's true of you now that you're in Christ—whether you're actually experiencing it or not—is the New Man that you've become. This is the real you that God looks at.

Now, in actual behavior, all things haven't become new yet. We still have many of the same old hangups and soul-kinks we had before we were born again. But the reason God calls us New Men is that He always looks at us in the light of the finished product He's making us into. And this attitude of God toward man has a creative power in it that actually brings our behavior into line with the way God sees us.

Paul talks about this New Man in Romans 7. He calls it "I," which is the translation of the word Greek *ego*. Freudian psychology has made the word "ego" familiar to us and it generally has the connotation of "self-centeredness." In the unregenerate man, the "ego" *is* totally self-centered because self is the primary thing that man is interested in.

But Paul uses the word *ego* in Romans 7 to refer to the man that God says he now is, the New Man in Christ. He says this New Man hates to sin, but unfortunately he still finds himself sinning. He laments that his New Man wants to do good, but somehow doesn't seem to have the power to perform the good it wants to do.

He finally concludes that even though he's a New Man in Christ and God will always look at him that way, he's still got the old rebellious flesh with him and it still wants to control him and often does. It expresses itself through Paul's attitudes as well as his actions; sins of the flesh as well as the soul (*self*).

But Paul's despair in Romans 7 leads to his biggest discovery, one that could come only by personal experience. That is, the New Man has no power in itself to overcome sin and live for God; it has desire, but no ability to do what it desires.

Then he writes the whole eighth chapter of Romans to show what all of his defeat had taught him. And that is that the power of the New Man is in the indwelling Holy Spirit and *He* must be depended on by the believer in order to overcome sin and live for God.

He Won Our Victory — Now We Must Claim it

Regeneration takes place in the human spirit because that's the part of us that needs new life. But the repercussions take place throughout our whole being as our souls and bodies come under the rightful domination of the spirit again. This is the whole purpose in regeneration, to bring the original unity and harmony back into the relationship between the body, soul, and spirit of man.

From the moment we're born again, our spirits are

indwelt by the Holy Spirit of God, because He's the actual agent of our new life. In fact, Paul says that if anyone doesn't have the Spirit in him, he doesn't belong to Christ (Romans 8:9). But whether the Holy Spirit is allowed to fill (control) our soul and flesh is a matter of our personal decision. The soul still has free will, and it must decide moment by moment what will dominate the life—the Holy Spirit, living through our reborn spirit, or the flesh (sin).

It's to the free will in the souls of men that Paul makes his plea in Romans 6:11-13: *"Reckon yourselves* to be dead to sin. . . . *Do not* let sin reign in your mortal body. . . . *Do not go on presenting* the members of your body to sin as instruments of unrighteousness."

These are commands which can be ignored or followed, whichever the mind decides. Our responsibility is to *decide* to obey, and then the Spirit goes into action in us and pours the power into us to *do* what we've decided. We're never relieved of the responsibility of *deciding* to follow the Father's will, but the actual power *to do it* comes from the Holy Spirit. That's what Paul meant when he said, "For it is God who is at work in you, both to will and to do" (Philippians 2:13). The *willing* part comes from the presence of the New Nature within us, and the *doing* comes from the power of the indwelling Holy Spirit.

Obedience and the Spirit's Power

A lot of believers want the *power* to come before they move out in response to the commands of the Word. They want to see, feel, and experience the victory before they follow the command to get into the battle. That really amounts to walking by sight and not by faith, because faith only needs the *promise* that God has already gone before us and is in control of the situation. The flesh demands visible proof before it can believe.

This truth is often confusing to believers who are just beginning to learn to walk by faith. They don't want to run ahead of the Lord. So, when they read certain commands in the Word of what God says should be true in the life of believers, they wait for some strong motivation and almost physical "shove" from the Holy Spirit before they move into action.

As far as I can see, you can't steer a car unless it's moving, and the Holy Spirit can't force us into action unless we've already made the decision to step out into whatever we've had revealed to us as God's will. For instance, we know it's God's will that we love one another because His Word teaches that (John 13:34). He doesn't tell us to have the "emotion" of love for one another. He tells us to "love" one another, and that's a verb, something that you *do*, not something that you necessarily *feel*.

So how do we handle a situation where we find ourselves disliking someone? Do we ask the Spirit to give us the emotion of love for him or her and then keep on hating him until we suddenly have some divine spurt of love come to us?

No! I believe we already know it's God's will to *demonstrate* love to this person, not necessarily feel it. And we know that if God wills something, then He's already promised to back that up with His enabling power. So trusting Him to empower us to *show* him love, whether we "feel" it or not, we begin to demonstrate love to him in the same ways we do to those we really love. We don't bad-mouth him to others. We begin to be sensitive to his needs and try to look at things from his point of view. We take time to show him kindnesses, and we simply accept him in the same way that God has accepted us, His former enemies.

Now, as we do these things, our attitude is that since we're doing what Jesus has commanded us, then He must also take care of the consequences of our actions and turn our "demonstration" of love into a true "feeling" of love.

There's a three-step progression that's involved in this example and in how we relate to the hundreds of other commands in the Word: *trust, obey, expect.*

First, we simply *trust* that what God has called us to

do, or cease doing, represents His best and highest plan for us, because He loves us so much.

Secondly, in the light of that knowledge, and with the promise that what He's called us to do He'll give us the power to, we *obey* His will.

Thirdly, we *expect* Him to keep His end of the bargain and empower us to do that which we've moved into by faith.

The Two Kinds of Believers

Now, you'd think that once a man was born again, he'd be so thankful to have his relationship with God restored that he would gladly and consistently allow the Holy Spirit to dominate his whole being, and would walk by faith, moment by moment.

But such is not the case with a great many believers. The soul (*self*) has held sway over us for so many years, that there's a lot of unlearning and relearning to do. Our minds must be renewed, as Paul tells us in Romans 12:2, in order that we might be transformed in our behavior. We've already been transformed on the inside because of the new birth. So now what we need to do is bring our behavior in line with what God says He's already made us. And that's where the need for the power of the Holy Spirit comes in. *We* can't transform ourselves, but the Holy Spirit can as He applies the cleansing and renewing power of the Word of God to our lives.

This, of course, necessitates that we spend time reading and studying the Bible. For as the Psalmist prayed, "Thy Word I have treasured in my heart, that I may not sin against Thee" (Psalm 119:11).

A believer who's consistently allowing himself to be renewed in his mind and has his human spirit in the dominant role in his life, allowing the Holy Spirit to work in him through it, is said by Paul to be a "spiritual man" (1 Corinthians 3:1). This doesn't mean that he's a perfect, sinless man. But it does mean that the thing which generally characterizes him is a preoccupation with the things of God and the spirit. When he sins, he confesses it to God and quickly relates it to His forgiveness on the cross. Then he turns again to walking by faith and being available to the Lord for whatever He might have in mind for him.

But in 1 Corinthians 3, Paul describes another kind of believer. This one is still a babe in Christ, even though he may have been a true believer for years. He's all caught up with the things of this world, and he's still living like the old soulish man he used to be. The flesh is the dominant factor in his life, so Paul calls him "carnal," which means "fleshly."

Throughout the New Testament epistles, a picture comes together of the things that characterize a carnal believer. It would do us all good to check this list and see if too many of these things apply to us too consistently. All believers will have some of these things in their lives occasionally and yet they couldn't honestly be categorized as "carnal." But if *many* of these things are true of you, I sincerely urge you to consider the possibility that you may be a carnal believer and in need of confessing your sins and claiming the power of the Holy Spirit to cleanse and renew you.

Carnal Believers:

. . . argue and reason about most things

. . . are self-righteous and defensive about their actions

. . . can't concentrate on spiritual things for long

. . . are up and down emotionally

. . . are overly sensitive

. . . don't give thanks in all things

. . . are worriers

. . . are talkative, always having to be at the center of each conversation and usually dominate it

. . . give in to lust of the eyes; are always buying things

. . . have an unbalanced emphasis on sex

. . . have a poor prayer life

. . . are undisciplined

. . . are easily discouraged

. . . when it comes to preaching, can't rely wholly on God, but fill up their sermons with illustrations, stories, and jokes

. . . are proud, because self is their center

. . . thrive on the sensational, because they're not sure people will be duly impressed with them if they don't

. . . are critical of fellow believers

. . . have a poor family life

. . . are braggers

. . . engage in frivolous and suggestive jesting

. . . are intemperate in eating and drinking

. . . indulge in swearing and dirty talk

. . . have no desire for the Word

. . . give in to jealousy and strife

Paul sums up the carnal believer's problem by saying, "You're walking like mere men" (1 Corinthians 3:3b).

And there's the tragedy, because believers aren't like "mere men." "Mere men" aren't all there. They have only a body and a soul; their spirits are nonfunctioning—dead. They're not *normal* human beings, but they don't realize it because everyone else they know is just like them.

Except true believers who walk by faith, allowing their spirits to have the rightful role of dominance in their lives. These are the "normal" people of the world because that's how God made man to function in the first place, and neither man nor God is truly happy until he does.

Summing it All Up

When the subject of regeneration is taught, it's usually related just to the work of God in giving new life to our dead human spirits and imparting the Holy Spirit to dwell in us. I hope you've been able to see from this chapter that there's much more than this involved in the complete work of regeneration. It's actually the work of God giving balance and harmony to the whole man once again. The spirit of man is put back into its rightful place of dominance in us, and the soul and flesh, that had gotten so out of hand with no inner restraint, are gradually brought back under the authority of the Holy Spirit, who dwells in our human spirit.

So regeneration means God has made us whole people again and by virtue of that fact has equipped us to live victoriously in this life and gloriously with Him for eternity.

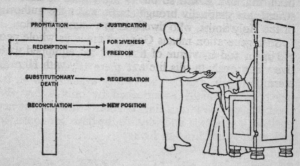

PROPITIATION ──→ JUSTIFICATION

REDEMPTION ──→ FOR GIVENESS / FREEDOM

SUBSTITUTIONARY DEATH ──→ REGENERATION

RECONCILIATION ──→ NEW POSITION

Chapter Eighteen

New Position

We've come now to the last chapter of the book, and it seems right that we should close this study of what Jesus Christ has done for man by looking at the incredible NEW POSITION that His reconciliation has given us. I'm convinced this subject is understood by few believers and that's why the church today as a whole doesn't have the vitality and power of the first-century church.

In the last hundred years a number of books have appeared which have dealt with this concept in one way or another. The believer's new position in Christ has made possible an intimate relationship with Him which has been called by many names: the Deeper Life, the Abiding Life, the Higher Life, the Crucified Life, the Exchanged Life, the Spirit-filled Life, the Victorious Life, the Faith-Rest Life, the Baptism of the Spirit, Identification With Christ, and Union With Christ.

Such writers as Jesse Penn Lewis, Ruth Paxson, Fritz Huegel, Charles Trumbell, E. W. Kenyon, Watchman Nee, Major Ian Thomas, L. S. Chafer, Miles Stanford, and Andrew Murray are among those many whose pens have given great clarity and insight into the liberating results of the believer's new position in Christ.

No matter what name we choose to call it, however, there can be little doubt that there is a life of great spiritual depth, power, and victory available to all believers, yet actually experienced by only a few. We want to examine in this final chapter just what our new position is in Christ and why it's the basis for consistent and victorious Christian living.

The Search for the "Deeper" Life

You don't have to be a believer for long before you discover by personal experience that *being* a Christian and *living* like one are often different things. Like the Apostle Paul in Romans 7, we find that we want to do the right thing but too often end up doing the very thing we hate.

When the realization of this conflict in our dual nature hits many believers, they simply don't feel like fighting it, and they give in to the up-and-down Christian life and settle into spiritual mediocrity. Others who are fighters by nature set out to find the solution to living above the pull of the world, the flesh, and the devil.

Many of these sincere souls have been led on strange pilgrimages by well-meaning friends, looking for this "deeper" life, only to come away with no lasting answers and more frustration. That's because what they're looking for isn't located in some higher or deeper *place* or some *experience*. It's located in a person, Jesus Christ.

The *deeper, higher, victorious, abiding, exchanged, and Spirit-filled* life is not an elusive, wishful aspiration. It's simply a matter of living with the moment-by-moment awareness that because of my absolute oneness with Jesus in the eyes of God, all that He is, *I am.*

His victory over sin *is mine*. He's holy and blameless in the eyes of the Father and *so am I*. Satan no longer has any authority over Him, *and he doesn't over me either.* He's more than conqueror, and Paul tells me that *I am too*. Christ was crucified, buried, raised from the dead, and is now seated at God's right hand. In the mind of God, *each true believer went through these same experiences* with Christ *and is now seated in the heavenlies* in Christ, regardless of where his actual physical body may be located here on earth at the moment.

In other words, my new position in Christ gives me a *total* identification with Jesus in God's eyes. As He looks at the Son, He looks at me in the same way because He sees me *in* the Son and the Son *in* me. If I took a grimy piece of paper and inserted it into the pages of a book and closed it, that paper would be totally identified with the book and we could no longer see it, only the book. Because Christ removed the barriers separating God and man, the one who places faith in that as having been done for him personally is "inserted" into Christ and Christ into Him. What becomes true of the One becomes true of the other.

Why Don't I Live Like What I Am?

If you're an honest believer you're probably saying to yourself about now, "Well, God may say I'm holy and blameless, and victorious over sin and Satan because of my union with Christ, but it doesn't come out that way in my daily experience. There's something wrong somewhere!"

More than likely there *is* something wrong, and it probably has to do with a failure to understand the difference between your new eternal *position* in Christ and your daily *experience* of living the Christian life. One is what you are in God's estimation and the other is what you are in practice.

A clear distinction must be made between these two relationships which each believer has with Christ. Our new position or union with Christ is a *legal* status which we have with God, and it becomes absolutely true of us the instant we place saving faith in Christ and never changes. But our day-to-day living of the Christian life here in this world is the *experiential* side of redemption, and it varies from moment-to-moment, depending on whether we walk with the Spirit of God in control of us or let our flesh dominate us.

Our New Possessions and Blessings

Believers are the richest people in town! They're spiritual billionaires, if they only knew it. Paul tells us in Ephesians 1:3 that God "has blessed us with every spiritual blessing in the heavenly places in Christ." Now that's something to get excited about, but many believers don't. They'd rather have some "*physical* blessings down here in *earthly* places." That would be more realistic and practical, they feel. But this attitude is only indicative of the fact that they've never really seen that our "treasures are laid up in heaven" because that's where we actually are in God's mind. What we have down here is only temporary and will benefit us only for our threescore and ten and then someone else gets it.

Once we've been born again, we're citizens of heaven and eternal beings. We're only passing through here on earth and God doesn't want us to settle down and get too comfortable and complacent.

Dr. Lewis Chafer, founder of Dallas Theological Seminary, went through the Bible and counted thirty-three different spiritual blessings that become legally true of us the moment we believe.[1] These new possessions and positions are instantaneously and simultaneously declared to be ours at that moment.

In the previous chapters in this book we looked at some of those spiritual blessings; justification, forgiveness, freedom, regeneration, new nature, acceptance with God, new righteousness, reconciliation, no more

---

[1] Lewis Sperry Chafer, *Systematic Theology* vol. III (Dallas, Tex.: Dallas Seminary Press, 1948).

condemnation, peace with God, a standing in grace, and redemption. There are at least twenty-one more eternal possessions that were given to us in the one package of salvation, and the thrill of the Christian life is finding out what these are and beginning to enjoy them here and now, not by and by.

Our Two Relationships With Christ

I think the chart on the next page will help to give us a better perspective of the two relationships a believer has with Christ; his *positional* and his *experiential*. Another way of saying it is the *eternal* and the *temporal* (*related to the believer's earthly life*). I want you particularly to notice the different characteristics of these two relationships. Our eternal position is credited to us *in toto* at the moment of salvation. It can't be improved on and it can't be diminished in any way. It's eternal.

In case it isn't perfectly clear to you yet, what the Bible is saying is that once you've been born again you can *never* lose your salvation because this eternal position will never cease to be true of you. Your temporal experience may change from day to day as sin comes into your life, but your eternal position is a forever fact. What happen *to* you or *in* you in your daily walk with Christ can never change, in the slightest degree, your eternal relationship with Christ.

When you're born into your earthly family, you may be a winner or a loser in your behavior, but you're still a member of that family. There's no way to be unborn just because you don't measure up to the standards of your family. You may be disciplined for wrong behavior, but you won't be disowned.

Look at the chart carefully. The cross represents that moment when you believe in Christ's death on your behalf and are born again. At that instant the Holy Spirit puts you into a family relationship with Christ which has two aspects to it, the eternal, invisible one in

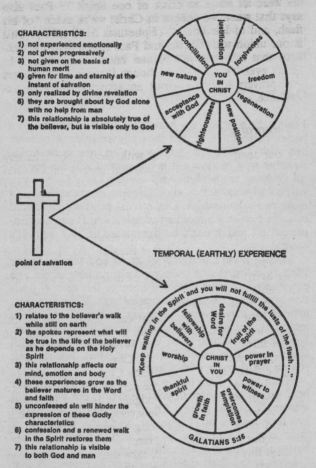

ETERNAL POSITION AND POSSESSIONS

CHARACTERISTICS:

1) not experienced emotionally
2) not given progressively
3) not given on the basis of human merit
4) given for time and eternity at the instant of salvation
5) only realized by divine revelation
6) they are brought about by God alone with no help from man
7) this relationship is absolutely true of the believer, but is visible only to God

(Wheel labels: YOU IN CHRIST — justification, forgiveness, freedom, regeneration, new position, righteousness, acceptance with God, new nature, reconciliation)

point of salvation

TEMPORAL (EARTHLY) EXPERIENCE

CHARACTERISTICS:

1) relates to the believer's walk while still on earth
2) the spokes represent what will be true in the life of the believer as he depends on the Holy Spirit
3) this relationship affects our mind, emotion and body
4) these experiences grow as the believer matures in the Word and faith
5) unconfessed sin will hinder the expression of these Godly characteristics
6) confession and a renewed walk in the Spirit restores them
7) this relationship is visible to both God and man

(Wheel labels: CHRIST IN YOU — "Keep walking in the Spirit and you will not fulfill the lusts of the flesh..." desire for Word, fruit of the Spirit, power in prayer, power to witness, overcomes temptation, growth in faith, thankful spirit, worship, fellowship with believers; GALATIANS 5:16)

the heavenlies (where Christ sits) and the temporal (earthly) one while you're still alive here on earth.

The act of placing you into Christ is called the "baptism of the Spirit" in 1 Corinthians 12:13: "For by one Spirit we were all baptized into one body, whether Jews or Greeks, whether slaves or free, and we were all made to drink of one Spirit." [2] Paul also says that when we believe in Christ we're made "of his flesh, and of His bones" (Ephesians 5:30 KJV). This is our union with Christ, and Paul likens it to the oneness that a man and woman enter in marriage. In God's eyes it's a fact even though it takes a lot of tears and prayers to bring about an actual oneness in experience.

Temporal Fellowship

By our temporal fellowship with God I don't in any way mean "temporary." Temporal simply means that which relates to time and space and in this case refers to the daily fellowship we experience with Christ. At the moment we're born again, not only are we placed into *Christ,* but He is placed into *us,* into our revived human spirits, and we come alive spiritually. His dwelling in us is to equip us to live here in this life until He comes to get us or we go home by death. He puts the Holy Spirit in us to empower us to live the kind of life He wants for us.

In the lower circle of the chart I've shown just a few of the new characteristics that can be expected in the life of a believer who submits to the empowering of Christ through the Holy Spirit. When we yield to temptation and subsequently to sin, Christ doesn't leave us, but the flesh or old self replaces Christ as the controlling influence in the life. If we stay in this condition for any length of time without judging it as sin and turning from it, we become carnal believers. But confessing our sin and once again authorizing Christ to take control restore our fellowship with Him.

With these things in mind, take time now to examine the chart. Notice particularly the eternal, permanent nature of our position in Christ. You'll see also that while we're still here on earth, Christ is to be the center

---

[2] For a fuller study of the baptism of the Holy Spirit see the appendix of the author's book, *Satan Is Alive and Well on Planet Earth* (Grand Rapids: Zondervan Publishing House, 1972).

of our lives, but it's the Holy Spirit who puts Him there
as we walk in total dependence on Him to do so.

How Do I Make My "Position" My "Experience"?

When God planned man's reconciliation, He obviously
didn't mean for us to be holy and victorious in our
"position" and weak and defeated in our "experience."
His plan has always been that our position and experience be brought into line with each other. But this
can happen only by our finding out how fantastic our
heavenly Father is and what He's made us to be because of our union with Christ in His death, burial,
resurrection, and ascension to the Father's right hand.

In this regard I always think of a story I heard once,
similar to Mark Twain's *The Prince and the Pauper,*
which beautifully illustrates this point.

One day the King and Queen of a far-off country
were bringing their new little Prince home from the
royal hospital when their carriage collided with a poor
pauper's cart. In this humble vehicle the poor man was
bringing his wife and new baby home from the mid-
wife's house. In the confusion of the moment, the two
couples picked up the wrong babies by mistake and the
little Prince went home to be raised by the pauper and
his wife.

As this baby grew into childhood, he was forced to
go into the streets and beg for food. Unknown to him,
of course, the very streets he begged on belonged to
him because they were the property of his true father.
Day after day he would go to the palace and look
through the iron fence at the little boy playing there
and he would say to himself, "Oh, if only *I* were a
Prince." Which, of course, he was, but he wasn't aware
of it.

All his life he lived in poverty and want because he
didn't know who he really was since he didn't know
"who" his father was.

Believers Live Like Spiritual Paupers

But do you know that millions of true believers are doing the same thing? They've never taken the time to find out "who" their real Father is, the King of Kings and Lord of Lords. They don't realize they're royal heirs to a royal throne. They're living in self-imposed spiritual poverty and cheating themselves of the experience of the riches of God's grace. I say the "experience" of them, because the riches are theirs whether they enjoy them or not.

I read not long ago about a man who lived like a bum for many years. He had been left a huge sum of money, but the authorities couldn't locate him. They traced him from flophouse to flophouse and finally found him asleep on a fifty-cents-a-night cot in a mission. He was then informed of His inheritance. He'd been rich for years but never knew it. He had lived needlessly as a tramp.

When I read that I thought, "What a waste of all those years." And that's just how I feel when I think of all the wasted years of happiness and spiritual service that go down the drain because "believers" are "unbelievers" when it comes to taking God at His word when He tells them *who* they are because of *whose* they are.

When we fail to live in the reality of our new position, daily experiencing the forgiveness, freedom, acceptance, and empowering of the Spirit (*just to name a few of our spiritual riches*), we short-change not only God, but ourselves and those whose lives we touch who so desperately need to see the reality of God in a human life.

Our "Position" is the Basis of All Victory

I said at the beginning of this chapter that knowing and counting on our new position in Christ is the basis of all victorious and consistent Christian living. Why do I say that?

It's because there's no other way to be set free from

the *power* of the Law, the sin nature, and Satan. In Romans 1–5, Paul lays out the *redemptive* work of Christ and shows us that it's our remedy for the *penalty* of sins. But in chapters 6–8 of Romans we see our complete identification with Christ in His death, burial, and resurrection and discover that that's the remedy for overcoming the *power* of sin.

Without the *power* of sin being dealt with in our lives, we'd be helpless victims of Satan's wiles and our own fleshly lusts, even though we are born again. There'd be no hope of deliverance from depression, defeat, discouragement, failure, and doubt.

But praise God, His plan for our *complete* salvation includes a means of victory over sin's power, and that's our co-crucifixion and resurrection with Jesus Christ.

The "Old Man" is Dead! Good Riddance!

In chapter sixteen, the chapter on Freedom, I told an amplified version of the allegory Paul uses in Romans 7:1-4. This was about a woman, who was married to a perfectionist tyrant and who could never satisfy his demands for perfection. Therefore she lived under constant condemnation. She finally met someone who was everything her husband was in the way of being perfect, but he was filled with love and concern for her. She wanted to be joined to him, but the law said she would be an adulteress if she left her husband. She could be rid of her domineering mate if he would die, but he was in perfect health; so the only other solution was for *her* to die, thereby effecting a legal separation from her husband. Then she would be free to marry anyone she chose. So she allowed her new lover to put her to death and then raise her back to life again and was joined in marriage to him.

This allegory is a fantastic application of the truths taught in Romans 6, 7, and 8. When you understand what the people in the allegory represent, the picture of your union with Christ in His death, burial, and resurrection will begin to unfold, and you'll be able to see how the cross has set you free.

The tyrannical husband represents the Law, but by application includes the sin nature and Satan. The woman is you, the believer. The "other man" is Jesus.

The Law, sin, and Satan will never die as far as their relationship to us is concerned here in this life. So the solution which God arrived at was to crucify us with Jesus, thus legally breaking our relationship to these tyrants. Then when Jesus rose from the dead, since in God's mind we were there in the grave with Him, we rose into a new life too, the same life that Jesus now lives, a life of total victory over the enemies of our soul.

On the basis of this legal severance of relationship, the authority of the old sin nature, the Law, and Satan have been forever broken over us, Christ's bride. As far as these things are concerned, we're dead to them. They can't legally touch us for a second unless we fail to realize and claim our freedom in Christ.

Out of Adam, Into Christ

To be in complete union with Christ is to have been legally taken out of our relationship to the first Adam and his ruin and placed into the Last Adam, Jesus, and thus made a partaker of all that He is. Both Adam and Christ demonstrate the principle that many can be affected for good or evil by one person's deed.

In Romans 5:12-21 Paul shows this analogy between Adam and Christ—the mess that Adam got mankind into and the means by which Christ got us out of it. He says sin entered the race through Adam, but we were forgiven our sins through Christ. Death came by Adam's transgression, but life came to us by Christ's obedience. Our relationship to the first Adam made us dead *in* sin, but our crucifixion with Christ made us dead *to* sin. Our identification with Christ completely removes the effect of our identification with Adam.

When we're born again, the baptism of the Holy Spirit is that ministry of the Spirit which takes us out of Adam and puts us into union with Christ. In fact, the word *baptism* means to totally identify one thing with another. It's the Greek word, *baptizo*, and it was never even translated into English from the original Greek; it was transliterated (which means to take the phonetics of a foreign word and make it a word in English). If we were to translate the word *baptizo* into its English equivalent, it would be the word "identification." So every time you read the word *baptized* in the Bible, you can mentally substitute the words *identified with* and you'll have a better understanding of the true meaning of this sometimes misunderstood word.

He Died for What I "Am" and What I've "Done"

We learned in the early chapters of this book that Christ bore our sins while He hung on the cross. In doing that He judged our sinful *deeds* and removed them as a barrier to God. But now we see that not only were our *sins* on Christ while He was on the cross, but because we have been so totally identified (baptized) with Christ in the mind of God, *we ourselves* were also hanging there on the cross with Jesus.

By taking *us* to the cross with Him and then into the grave, He forever put to death not only our sinful *deeds,* but our sinful *selves,* thus removing not only what we did, but what we *were* (hostile to God, unrighteous, etc.) as a barrier between ourselves and God. He's provided *forgiveness* for what we've *done* and *deliverance* from what we *are.*

Now, not only are my sins not offensive to God, but I'm not either. I'm so accepted by the Father, because of my union with Christ, that in His mind He sees me as actually being seated in heaven in Christ. Paul emphasized this when he wrote, "But God, being rich in mercy, because of His great love with which He loved us, even when we were dead in our transgressions, made us alive together with Christ . . . and raised us up with Him, and seated us with Him in the heavenly places in Christ Jesus" (Ephesians 2:4-6).

Identified With Christ From the Cross to the Throne

The key that unlocks the hidden truth of our release from Satan and the sin nature's power is the little preposition "with." We died *with* Christ, were buried *with* Him, resurrected *with* Him, are seated *with* Him, and will eventually reign *with* Him (Romans 6:1-13; Colossians 3:1-3; Revelation 20:6). Our entire ground for victory as a believer is wrapped up in the death-dealing blow that the death, burial, resurrection, and ascension of Jesus gave to the authority and power of Satan and sin.[3] If you understood no other truths in the Bible than these and fully grasped your total identification with Christ in this victory, you'd be equipped to live victoriously over Satan and over the constant lure and pull of the flesh.

No Need to be Crucified Daily: Once Was Enough!

In one beautiful, all-inclusive statement in Galatians 2:20 Paul sums up the finality and the purpose of our crucifixion with Christ: "I *have been* crucified with Christ; and it is no longer I who live, but Christ lives in me; and the life which I now live in the flesh I live by faith in the Son of God, who loved me, and delivered Himself up for me."

Notice that Paul is careful to point out that our crucifixion with Christ is already a fact, not something which I must do to myself daily or try to get Christ to do to me at some point in my Christian life. In Romans 6, each time Paul speaks of our identification with Christ in His death, he uses the past tense of the verb:

---

[3] For a fuller understanding of this subject, see chapter fourteen of the author's book, *Satan Is Alive and Well on Planet Earth*.

"we *have been* buried with Him (verse 4); "we *have become* united with Him in the likeness of His death" (verse 5); "our old self *was crucified* with Him" (verse 6); "we *have died* with Christ" (verse 8).

Then Paul makes the powerful statement in Romans 6:9-11 that on the basis of our *having been* crucified with Christ, we ourselves are actually as dead to sin's power as Jesus is, since His victory over it is ours also. Obviously it goes without saying that if we haven't let it become a reality to us that we've been identified with Christ in His death and resurrection, then we won't see Christ's victory as ours and consequently won't reckon ourselves dead to sin's power in our daily lives. We'll valiantly struggle against temptation out of a genuine desire not to sin; but without knowing that we have legitimate grounds for claiming complete immunity to its power, we'll eventually wear down in our defenses and give in and sin.

We Died in Order to Live!

Knowing that we've been made dead to sin is only half the necessary information that leads to daily victorious Christian living. The other half of the co-crucifixion fact is that we've been made alive with Christ in order to experience the same newness of life that's His. This is called "resurrection life," and it's totally free from any domination of Satan, sin, self, the flesh, and the Law of God.

In Romans 6:11 Paul urges believers to "consider yourselves to be dead to sin, but alive to God in Christ Jesus." Couple this with his statement in Galatians 2:20 that he had been "crucified with Christ," nevertheless was still alive, and it looks like a contradiction. How can you be both dead and alive at the same time? The answer to that is found in that same verse: "It is no longer I who live, but Christ lives in me; and the life which I now live in the flesh I live by faith in the Son of God." We're judicially declared dead to sin's power, but it only becomes a reality in our lives as we consider it to be a fact and by faith count on Christ to live His life in and through us.

Why Are These "Co-Crucifixion" Truths Hard to Grasp!

I'm under no illusions that everyone who has read the words in this last vital chapter has understood the depth of them. For 2,000 years these liberating truths have been prominent in Paul's teachings, particularly in Romans 6, 7, 8 and Galatians and Colossians, yet few believers have grasped their reality in the daily experience of coping with temptation and the lusts of the flesh.

Why is this so?

I believe there are several reasons. First of all, as much as some believers would like it, there are no shortcuts to spiritual maturity just as there are no short-cuts to emotional and physical maturity. Time and the experience of trial and error go into preparing us for an acceptance of these deeper life truths. If we have any notion that there's even the least little thing we can do in ourselves to improve our status with God and strengthen ourselves against the power of sin, then we'll miss God's solution. I can't begin to tell you of the countless believers I've known, including myself, who, not knowing of our co-crucifixion with Christ, set out on rigorous programs of Bible study, prayer, seeking to walk in the Spirit, witnessing, Scripture memorization, and a variety of other good, religious activities in an effort to fortify themselves against sin and Satan's power.

In nearly every case the results have been the same. At first, it seemed to help, but gradually what had been done with a sense of joy and enthusiasm began to be a drag and legalistic ritual. When all these good spiritual deeds failed to keep us from yielding to sin's power, we were driven to frustration. And that's where far too many believers spend most of their Christian lives, with conscious or subconscious frustration and discouragement because they know they've tried the formulas that sincere ministers and friends have suggested and they haven't worked.

If you've come to the point where you haven't any more tricks left up your sleeve for living victoriously over sin and your old self, then there's one of three things you can do: settle down in your defeat and live openly in the flesh with no pretense of trying to be godly or spiritual; or reluctantly come to the conclusion that there isn't any real victory available but try to keep up a spiritual front so as not to be a bad testimony to others; or thank God that He's finally revealed the path to victorious Christian living to you, the path of your co-crucifixion with Christ to sin's power, and begin to reckon it daily to be a fact in your life. Only then can the resurrected life of Christ—the Spirit-filled life —be consistently manifest through you. And only then can you say No to temptation and yield your new self to God and fully expect to be delivered from sin's power.

Believers Need to be "Son" Conscious

Another reason why believers fail to grasp the reality of their emancipation from sin's power is because so much preaching and teaching today is centered around our sinfulness and not around Christ's forgiveness of it. If we're "sin" conscious continually, then we can't be "Son" conscious. Sin-consciousness only leads us to self-condemnation and self-effort to overcome the sin. But Son-consciousness continually reminds us of God's love and acceptance of us and the forgiveness which He purchased at the cross.

Let's take a practical look at this concept. Nearly every believer has some area of his life where he feels God would like him to change. It may be a habit that isn't consistent with a Christian testimony or it may be an inner attitude of bitterness, jealousy, or lust. Much time is spent in self-recrimination and anger at our inability to give up this sin. In fact, we're so absorbed in our problem that we have little time to focus on the problem-solver, Jesus. And because we're consumed with the consciousness of how sinful and unfaithful we

are, we fail to appreciate the forgiveness and faithful-
ness of God toward us. Our sin-consciousness will always lead us to some kind of *human* effort to change
our behavior and that path is doomed to failure since
that's simply the flesh trying to change itself.

What's the solution, then, to applying the work of
the cross to our daily lives? How can we be consistently
reminded to reckon ourselves dead to sin and alive to
God? And what are the practical results that we can
expect in our lives as we walk by faith, with the resurrection life of Christ manifesting itself through our
emotions and behavior?

Only a Renewed Mind Can Grasp These Co-Crucifixion Truths

When you come into the family of God by your rebirth, you bring with you the accumulation of attitudes,
behavior, outlook, complexes, and experiences of perhaps years of living without Christ and His influence.
All these have combined to make you the person you
are. Now suddenly the Bible tells you that you're a
"new creation" in Christ. "The old has passed away,
behold, the new has come." God also says He now sees
you as "holy and blameless" in His eyes because you're
"hidden in Christ" and all He sees is Him (2 Corinthians 5:17; Colossians 1:22; 3:3).

The question now is, how do you make what God
says is true of you to be more real in your mind than
what you know yourself to be on the basis of your past
performance? You know you've been anything but
holy and blameless, and there are probably a number
of things in your life you haven't been able to forgive
yourself for, let alone accept God's forgiveness for.

There's only one answer. You must have your mind
flushed of the lingering consciousness of the old self-
life and a whole new viewpoint of yourself put in its
place. You must have your mind renewed before your
behavior can change.

How does this take place?

Paul says in Romans 12:2 that the only way to be

transformed and not conform to the old way you used to behave is to have your mind renewed. Then the psalmist tells us how this is done: "How can a young man keep his way pure? By keeping it according to Thy word. . . . Thy word I have treasured in my heart that I may not sin against Thee" (Psalm 119:9, 11).

There's no way to have our minds renewed apart from the cleansing and nurturing power of God's Word. The writer of Hebrews calls the Word "milk" and "meat" because it's that which gives us growth and understanding (Hebrews 5:12-14 KJV). Countless believers are struggling along trying to kep their heads above water spiritually, and in almost every case with which I've had to counsel, they had no regular intake of the Word or Christian literature or tapes. There's just no way to find out about the incredible new person you've been made to be apart from the revelation of it in God's Word. You won't be consistently reminded to reckon yourself dead to the flesh and Satan's temptings unless you saturate your mind with God's viewpoint of you.

Your "New Self" Means That You Can Have a New Self-image

The world, the flesh, and the devil don't let up on you just because you've been born again. In fact, that's when they really go to work trying to keep you from finding out your new authority over them so you won't give them a hard time. They'll particularly conspire together to keep you conscious of all your faults and failures so you'll never come to see the brand new creation God has made you into. If you're full of a sense of inferiority before God, you'll never be greatly used by Him because you won't believe He can use someone like you conceive yourself to be.

In the new science of psycho-cybernetics, the study of self-image, it's been conclusively demonstrated that you can't act consistently contrary to your own self-image—that which you conceive yourself to be. Every person has developed an image of himself over his years of growing up, and unless there is a radical intervention at some point which changes him in some way, physically, emotionally or spiritually, he'll be able to act only in accordance with what he believes he is.

Dr. Maxwell Maltz, a plastic surgeon who had years of experience at observing people's preoperative and postoperative self-images, said in his book *Psychocybernetics* that even after dramatic surgery which erased ugly disfigurements, some people still behaved as though they looked the same. They simply could not stop believing they weren't the same old ugly person. Their self-image was so deeply ingrained that they had built their whole life out of it, and it was virtually impossible for them to conceive of themselves as being or looking any different.

Yet he observed a definite phenomenon in other patients. Within several weeks after the plastic surgery had removed an ugly scar, large nose, or similarly unattractive feature, some patients began to experience a change in their whole personalities and behavior. Those who had previously let their disfigurement give them an inferiority complex began to be very self-confident and outgoing. Others who had been failures in one thing or another began to see themselves as winners, and when they did, they actually became more successful in their endeavors.

From twenty years of observing this, Dr. Maltz rightly concluded that it's impossible to behave consistently differently from what you see yourself to be.

But as startling as this discovery was to the field of science, it's a principle as old as the Bible. This is the heart of what it means to be a "new creation" in Christ. When I began to live with the intimate awareness of my new position in Christ, seated far above this old corrupt earth at the right hand of God and viewed as holy and blameless in His eyes, then I'll begin to behave like the royal heir to the royal throne which God says I am. As I let the Holy Spirit renew my mind through God's Word to really see my union with Christ in His defeat of Satan, demons, sin, the world, and my old corrupted self, then and only then will I begin to be transformed into His image and likeness while I'm still here on this earth.

My *self*-image can be permanently improved only when I realize that I've got a whole new *self* inside of me. That new self is beautiful to God because He created it. I don't need to be afraid to have men or God look deeply into me because I know what they'll see. They'll see God's handiwork, not in its finished form, but nevertheless perfect in His eyes. It's a great feeling to like your "self" and not be afraid to be transparent.

A Closing Word of Personal Testimony

I began this book with my personal story of the miracle of God's finding me and putting me into His forever family. One of my main purposes in writing this book has been to show God's great Father's-heart in providing a way to reconcile all of mankind back to Himself.

But I have wanted to show Christ not only as our reconciler, but also as the healer of broken hearts and damaged lives. No one could have been more fouled up in his personal life then I was. My self-image was so rotten that I often contemplated suicide because I felt the world would be better off without someone like me. Even after I became a true believer in Christ I was often inhibited from being available for God's use because I felt so unworthy. I even felt it was spiritual to feel unworthy of God's love and acceptance.

It wasn't until I began to learn about my new exalted position in Christ and the thirty-three new possessions and eternal endowments He had conferred upon me that I began to feel like a different person. No one else had ever thought so highly of me. As I began to find out more and more about this great God who had loved me so much that He put me into union with His Son, I had a greater and greater appreciation of *who* I was because of *whose* I was. My Father was a King, so that made me a royal prince.

As you've read this book, my sincere hope has been

that you've seen Jesus and yourself in a whole new light. If you've needed to be reconciled to God, I pray that you have been. If you've needed to be liberated from a quagmire of self-life and defeat, I trust you've seen the provision God has made for your liberation at the cross.

You were made to soar, not crawl. In Christ you're lifted above the stain and fetters of sin on the "wings of eagles." Settle back now and begin to enjoy this "so great salvation."